The Life of George Washington

G. WASHINGTON.

THE LIFE

OF

GEORGE WASHINGTON;

WITH

CURIOUS ANECDOTES,

EQUALLY HONOURABLE TO HIMSELF,

AND

EXEMPLARY TO HIS YOUNG COUNTRYMEN.

A life how useful to his country led!
How loved! while living!—how revered! now dead!
Lisp! lisp! his name, ye children yet unborn!
And with like deeds your own great names adorn.

EMBELLISHED WITH SIX ENGRAVINGS.

BY M. L. WEEMS,

FORMERLY RECTOR OF MOUNT VERNON PARISH.

The author has treated this great subject with admirable " success in a new way. He turns all the actions of Washington, to the encouragement of virtue, by a careful application of numerous exemplifications drawn from the conduct of the founder of our republic from his earliest life."

H. LEE, *Major-General, Army U. S.*

PHILADELPHIA:

PUBLISHED BY JOSEPH ALLEN,

AND SOLD BY GRIGG AND ELLIOT,

No. 9, North Fourth Street.

....

1840.

COPY RIGHT SECURED ACCORDING TO LAW.

Philadelphia:
King & Baird, Printers,
No. 9 George St.

THE LIFE

OF

WASHINGTON.

CHAPTER I.

Oh! as along the stream of time thy name
Expanded flies, and gathers all its fame;
May then these lines to future days descend,
And prove thy COUNTRY's good thine only end!

"Ah, gentlemen!"—exclaimed Bonaparte—'twas just as he was about to embark for Egypt—some young Americans happening at Toulon, and anxious to see the mighty Corsican, had obtained the honour of an introduction to him. Scarcely were past the customary salutations, when he eagerly asked, "how fares your countryman, the great WASHINGTON?" "He was very well," replied the youths, brightening at the thought, that they were the countrymen of Washington; "he was very well, general, when we left America."—"Ah, gentlemen!" rejoined he, "Washington can never be otherwise than well.—The measure of his fame is full.—Posterity will talk of him with reverence as the founder of a great empire, when my name shall be lost in the vortex of Revolutions!"

Who, then, that has a spark of virtuous curiosity, but must wish to know the history of him whose name could thus awaken the sigh even of Bonaparte? But is not his history already known? Have not a

1*

thousand orators spread his fame abroad, bright as his own Potomac, when he reflects the morning sun, and flames like a sea of liquid gold, the wonder and delight of all the neighbouring shores ? Yes, they have indeed spread his fame abroad. ... his fame as Generalissimo of the armies, and first President of the councils of his nation. But this is not half his fame. ... True, he has been seen in greatness : but it is only the greatness of public character, which is no evidence of true greatness ; for a public character is often an artificial one. At the head of an army or nation, where gold and glory are at stake, and where a man feels himself the burning focus of unnumbered eyes ; he must be a paltry fellow, indeed, who does not play his part pretty handsomely. ... even the common passions of pride, avarice, or ambition, will put him up to his mettle, and call forth his best and bravest doings. But let this heat and blaze of public situation and incitement be withdrawn ; let him be thrust back into the shade of private life ; and you shall see how soon, like a forced plant robbed of its hot-bed, he will drop his false foliage and fruit, and stand forth confessed in native stickweed sterility and worthlessness.—There was Benedict Arnold— while strutting a BRIGADIER GENERAL on the public state, he could play you the great man, on a handsome scale——he out-marched Hannibal, and out-fought Burgoyne——he chased the British like curlews, or cooped them up like chickens ! and yet in the private walks of life, in Philadelphia, he could swindle rum from the commissary's stores, and, with the aid of loose women, retail it by the gill ! !—And there was the great duke of Marlborough too—his public character, a thunderbolt in war ! Britian's boast, and the terror of the French ! But his private character, what ? Why a swindler to whom Arnold's self could hold a candle ; a perfect nondescript of baseness ; a shaver of farthings from the poor sixpenny pay of his own brave soldiers ! !

It is not, then, in the glare of public, but in the shade of private life, that we are to look for the man. Private life, is always real life. Behind the curtain, where the eyes of the million are not upon him, and where a man can have no motive but inclination, no incitement but honest nature, there he will always be sure to act himself: consequently, if he act greatly, he must be great indeed. Hence it has been justly said, that, "our private deeds, if noble, are noblest of our lives."

Of these private deeds of Washington very little has been said. In most of the elegant orations pronounced to his praise, you see nothing of Washington below the clouds—nothing of Washington the dutiful son—the affectionate brother—the cheerful school-boy—the diligent surveyor—the neat draftsman—the laborious farmer—the widow's husband—the orphan's father—the poor man's friend. No! this is not the Washington you see; 'tis only Washington, the HERO, and the Demigod—Washington the sun-beam in council, or the storm in war.

And in all the ensigns of character amidst which he is generally drawn, you see none that represent him what he really was, "the jupiter Conservator," the friend and benefactor of men. Where's his bright ploughshare that he loved—or his wheat-crowned fields, waving in yellow ridges before the wanton breeze—or his hills whitened over with flocks—or his clover covered pastures spread with innumerous herds—or his neat-clad servants with songs rolling the heavy harvest before them? Such were the scenes of peace, plenty, and happiness, in which Washington delighted. But his eulogists have denied him these, the only scenes which belong to man the GREAT; and have trick'd him up in the vile drapery of man the little. See! there he stands! with the port of Mars "the destroyer," dark frowning over the fields of war—the lightning of Potter's blade is by his side —the deep-mouthed cannon is before him, disgorg-

ing its flesh-mangling balls—his war-horse pants
with impatience to bear him, a speedy thunderbolt,
against the pale and bleeding ranks of Britain!—
These are the drawings usually given of Washington;
drawings masterly no doubt, and perhaps justly
descriptive of him in some scenes of his life. But
scenes they were, which I am sure his soul abhorred,
and in which, at any rate, you see nothing of his
private virtues. These old fashioned commodities
are generally thrown into the back ground of the
picture; and treated, as the grandees at the London
and Paris routs, treat their good old aunts and grand-
mothers, huddling them together into the back rooms,
there to wheeze and cough by themselves, and not
depress the fine laudanum-raised spirits of the young
sparklers. And yet it was to those old fashioned virtues that our hero owed every thing. For they in
fact were the food of the great actions of him, whom
men call Washington. It was they that enabled him,
first to triumph over himself; then over the British;
and uniformly to set such bright examples of human
perfectibility and true greatness, that, compared there-
with, the history of his capturing Cornwallis and
Tarleton, with their buccaneering legions, sounds
almost as small as the story of General Putnam's
catching his wolf and her lamb-killing whelps.

Since then it is the private virtues that lay the
foundation of all human excellence—since it was
these that exalted Washington to be "Columbia's
first and greatest Son," be it our first care to present
these, in all their lustre, before the admiring eyes
of our children. To them his private character is
every thing; his public, hardly any thing. For how
glorious soever it may have been in Washington to
have undertaken the emancipation of his country;
to have stemmed the long tide of adversity; to have
baffled every effort of a wealthy and warlike nation;
to have obtained for his countrymen the completest
victory, and for himself the most unbounded power;

and then to have returned that power, accompanied with all the weight of his own great character and advice to establish a government that should immortalize the blessings of liberty—however glorious, I say, all this may have been to himself, or instructive to future generals and presidents, yet does it but little concern our children. For who among us can hope that his son shall ever be called, like Washington, to direct the storm of war, or to ravish the ears of deeply listening Senates? To be constantly placing him then, before our children, in this high character, what is it but like springing in the clouds a golden Phœnix, which no mortal calibre can ever hope to reach? Or like setting pictures of the Mammoth before the mice, whom "not all the manna of Heaven" can ever raise to equality? Oh no! give us his private virtues! In these, every youth is interested, because in these every youth may become a Washington—a Washington in piety and patriotism,—in industry and honour—and consequently a Washington, in what alone deserves the name, SELF ESTEEM and UNIVERSAL RESPECT.

CHAPTER II.

BIRTH AND EDUCATION.

"Children like tender osiers take the bow;
"And as they first are form'd, forever grow."

To this day numbers of good Christians can hardly find faith to believe that Washington was, bona fide, a Virginian! "What! a buckskin! say they with a smile. "George Washington a buckskin! pshaw! impossible! he was certainly an European: So great a man could never have been born in America."

So great a man could never have been born in

America!—why that's the very prince of reasons
why he should have been born here! Nature, we
know, is fond of harmonies; and paria paribus, that
is, great things to great, is the rule she delights to
work by. Where, for example, do we look for the
whale, "the biggest born of nature?" not, 1 trow, in
a mill-pond, but in the main ocean. "There go the
great ships:" and there are the spoutings of whales
amidst their boiling foam.

By the same rule, where shall we look for Washington, the greatest among men, but in America—
that greatest Continent, which, rising from beneath
the frozen pole, stretches far and wide to the south,
running almost "the whole length of this vast terrene,"
and sustaining on her ample sides the roaring shock
of half the watery globe? And equal to its size is the
furniture of this vast continent, where the Almighty
has reared his cloud-capt mountains, and spread his
sea-like lakes, and poured his mighty rivers, and
hurled down his thundering cataracts in a style of
the sublime, so far superior to any thing of the kind
in the other continents, that we may fairly conclude
that great men and great deeds are designed for
America.

This seems to be the verdict of honest analogy;
and accordingly we find America the honoured cra-
dle of Washington, who was born on Pope's creek,
in Westmoreland county, Virginia, the 22nd of Feb-
ruary, 1732. His father, whose name was Augustin
Washington, was also a Virginian: but his grand-
father (John) was an Englishman, who came over
and settled in Virginia in 1657.

His father, fully persuaded that a marriage of
virtuous love comes nearest to angelic life, early
stepped up to the altar with glowing cheeks and joy
sparkling eyes, while by his side with soft warm
hand, sweetly trembling in his, stood the angel-form
of the lovely Miss Dandridge.

After several years of great domestic happiness,

Mr. Washington was separated by death from this excellent woman, who left him and two children to lament her early fate.

Fully persuaded still, that "it is not good for man to be alone," he renewed, for the second time, the chaste delights of matrimonial love. His consort was Miss Mary Ball, a young lady of fortune, and descended from one of the best families in Virginia.

From his intermarriage with this charming girl, it would appear that our hero's father must have possessed either a very pleasing person, or highly polished manners, or perhaps both; for, from what I can learn, he was at that time at least forty years old! while she, on the other hand, was universally toasted as the belle of the Northern Neck, and in the full bloom and freshness of love-inspiring sixteen. This I have from one who tells me that he has carried down many a sett dance with her; I mean that amiable and pleasant old gentleman, John Fitzhugh, Esq. of Stafford, who was, all his life, a neighbour and intimate of the Washington family. By his first wife, Mr. Washington had two children, both sons —Lawrence and Augustin. By his second wife, he had five children, four sons and a daughter—George, Samuel, John, Charles, and Elizabeth. Those over delicate folk, who are ready to faint at thought of a second marriage, might do well to remember, that the greatest man that ever lived was the son of this second marriage.

Little George had scarcely attained his fifth year, when his father left Pope's creek, and came up to a plantation which he had in Stafford, opposite to Fredericksburg. The house in which he lived is still to be seen. It lifts its low and modest front of faded red, over the turbid waters of Rappahannock; whither, to this day, numbers of people repair, and, with emotions unutterable, looking at the weather-beaten mansion, exclaim, "Here's the house where the great Washington was born!"

But it is all a mistake; for he was born, as I said, at Pope's creek, in Westmoreland county, near the margin of his own roaring Potomac.

The first place of education to which George was ever sent, was a little "old field school," kept by one of his father's tenants, named Hobby; an honest, poor old man, who acted in the double character of sexton and schoolmaster. On his skill as a grave-digger, tradition is silent; but for a teacher of youth, his qualifications were certainly of the humbler sort; making what is generally called an A. B. C. schoolmaster. Such was the preceptor who first taught Washington the knowledge of letters! Hobby lived to see his young pupil in all his glory, and rejoiced exceedingly. In his cups—for though a sexton, he would sometimes drink, particularly on the General's birth days—he used to boast, that "'twas he, who, between his keees, had laid the foundation of George Washington's greatness."

But though George was early sent to a schoolmaster, yet he was not on that account neglected by his father. Deeply sensible of the loveliness and worth of which human nature is capable, through the virtues and graces early implanted in the heart, he never for a moment, lost sight of George in those all-important respects.

To assist his son to overcome that selfish spirit, which too often leads children to fret and fight about trifles, was a notable care of Mr. Washington. For this purpose, of all the presents, such as cakes, fruit, &c. he received, he was always desired to give a liberal part to his play-mates. To enable him to do this with more alacrity, his father would remind him of the love which he would thereby gain, and the frequent presents which would in return be made to him; and also would tell of that great and good God, who delights above all things to see children love one another, and will assuredly reward them for acting so amiable a part.

Some idea of Mr. Washington's plan of education in this respect, may be collected from the following anecdote, related to me twenty years ago by an aged lady, who was a distant relative, and, when a girl, spent much of her time in the family:

"On a fine morning," said she, "in the fall of 1737, Mr. Washington having little George by the hand, came to the door and asked my cousin Washington and myself to walk with him to the orchard, promising he would show us a fine sight. On arriving at the orchard, we were presented with a fine sight indeed. The whole earth, as far as we could see, was strewed with fruit: and yet the trees were bending under the weight of apples, which hung in clusters like grapes, and vainly strove to hide their blushing cheeks behind the green leaves. Now, George, said his father, look here, my son! don't you remember when this good cousin of yours brought you that fine large apple last spring, how hardly I could prevail on you to divide with your brothers and sisters; though I promised you that if you would but do it, God Almighty would give you plenty of apples this fall. Poor George could not say a word; but hanging down his head, looked quite confused, while with his little naked toes he scratched in the soft ground. Now look up, my son, continued his father, look up, George! and see there how richly the blessed God has made good my promise to you. Wherever you turn your eyes, you see the trees loaded with fine fruit; many of them indeed breaking down; while the ground is covered with mellow apples, more than you could eat, my son, in all your life time."

George looked in silence on the wide wilderness of fruit. He marked the busy humming bees, and heard the gay notes of birds; then lifting his eyes, filled with shining moisture, to his father, he softly said, "Well, Pa, only forgive me this time; and see if I ever be so stingy any more."

Some, when they look up to the oak, whose giant

2

arms throw a darkening shade over distant acres, or whose single trunk lays the keel of a man of war, cannot bear to hear of the time when this mighty plant was but an acorn, which a pig could have demolished. But others, who know their value, like to learn the soil and situation which best produces such noble trees. Thus, parents that are wise, will listen, well pleased, while I relate how moved the steps of the youthful Washington, whose single worth far outweighs all the oaks of Bashan and the red spicy cedars of Lebanon. Yes, they will listen delighted while I tell of their Washington in the days of his youth, when his little feet were swift towards the nests of birds; or when, wearied in the chase of the butterfly, he laid him down on his grassy couch and slept, while ministering spirits, with their roseate wings, fanned his glowing cheeks, and kissed his lips of innocence with that fervent love which makes the Heaven!

Never did the wise Ulysses take more pains with his beloved Telemachus, than did Mr. Washington with George, to inspire him with an early-love of truth. "Truth, George," said he, "is the loveliest quality of youth. I would ride fifty miles, my son, to see the little boy whose heart is so honest, and his lips so pure, that we may depend on every word he says. O how lovely does such a child appear in the eyes of every body! his parents doat on him. His relations glory in him. They are constantly praising him to their children, whom they beg to imitate him. They are often sending for him to visit them; and receive him, when he comes, with as much joy as if he were a little angel, come to set pretty examples to their children.

"But, Oh! how different, George, is the case with the boy who is so given to lying, that nobody can believe a word he says! He is looked at with aversion wherever he goes, and parents dread to see him come among their children. Oh, George! my son! rather than see you come to this pass, dear as you are to my heart, gladly would I assist to nail you up in your little coffin, and follow you to your grave. Hard, indeed, would it be to me to give up my son, whose little feet are always so ready to run about with me, and whose fondly looking eyes, and sweet prattle make so large a part of my happiness. But still I would give him up, rather than see him a common liar."

"Pa," said George very seriously, "do I ever tell lies?"

"No, George, I thank God you do not, my son; and I rejoice in the hope you never will. At least, you shall never, from me, have cause to be guilty of so shameful a thing. Many parents, indeed, even compel their children to this vile practice, by barbarously beating them for every little fault: hence, on the next offence, the little terrified creature slips out a lie! just to escape the rod. But as to yourself George, you know I have always told you, and now tell you again, that, whenever by accident, you do any thing wrong, which must often be the case, as you are but a poor little boy yet, without experience or knowledge, you must never tell a falsehood to conceal it; but come bravely up, my son, like a little man, and tell me of it: and, instead of beating you, George, I will but the more honour and love you for it, my dear."

This, you'll say, was sowing good seed!—Yes, it was: and the crop, thank God, was, as I believe it ever will be, where a man acts the true parent, that is, the Guardian Angel, by his child.

The following anecdote is a case in point. It is too valuable to be lost, and too true to be doubted; for it was communicated to me by the same excellent lady to whom I am indebted for the last.

"When George," said she, "was about six years old, he was made the wealthy master of a hatchet! of which, like most little boys, he was immoderately

fond, and was constantly going about chopping every
thing that came in his way. One day, in the garden,
where he often amused himself hacking his mother's
pea-sticks, he unluckily tried the edge of his hatchet
on the body of a beautiful young English cherry-tree,
which he barked so terribly, that I don't believe the
tree ever got the better of it. The next morning the
old gentleman, finding out what had befallen his tree,
which, by the by, was a great favourite, came into
the house; and with much warmth asked for the
mischievous author, declaring at the same time, that
he would not have taken five guineas for his tree.
Nobody could tell him any thing about it. Presently
George and his hatchet made their appearance.
"George," said his father, "do you know who killed
that beautiful little cherry tree yonder in the garden?"
This was a tough question; and George staggered
under it for a moment; but quickly recovered himself: and looking at his father, with the sweet face of
youth brightened with the inexpressible charm of all-
conquering truth, he bravely cried out, "I can't tell
a lie, Pa; you know I can't tell a lie. I did cut it
with my hatchet."—Run to my arms, you dearest
boy, cried his father in transports, run to my arms;
glad am I, George, that you killed my tree; for you
have paid me for it a thousand fold. Such an act of
heroism in my son is more worth than a thousand
trees, though blossomed with silver, and their fruits
of purest gold."

It was in this way by interesting at once both his
heart and head, that Mr. Washington conducted
George with great ease and pleasure along the happy
paths of virtue. But well knowing that his beloved
charge, soon to be a man, would be left exposed to
numberless temptations, both from himself and from
others, his heart throbbed with the tenderest anxiety
to make him acquainted with that great being, whom
to know and love, is to possess the surest defence
against vice, and the best of all motives to virtue and

happiness. To startle George into a lively sense of his Maker, he fell upon the following very curious, but impressive expedient:

One day he went into the garden, and prepared a little bed of finely pulverized earth, on which he wrote George's name at full, in large letters—then strewing in plenty of cabbage seed, he covered them up, and smoothed all over nicely with the roller.—This bed he purposely prepared close along side of a gooseberry walk, which happening at this time to be well hung with ripe fruit, he knew would be honoured with George's visits pretty regularly every day. Not many mornings had passed away before in came George, with eyes wild rolling, and his little cheeks ready to burst with great news.

"O Pa! come here! come here!"

"What's the matter, my son? what's the matter?"

"O come here, I tell you, Pa : come here! and I'll shew you such a sight as you never saw in all your life time."

The old gentleman suspecting what George would be at, gave him his hand, which he seized with great eagerness, and tugging him along through the garden, led him point blank to the bed whereon was inscribed, in large letters, and in all the freshness of newly sprung plants, the full name of

GEORGE WASHINGTON.

"There Pa?" said George, quite in an ecstacy of astonishment, "did you ever see such a sight in all your life time?"

"Why it seems like a curious affair, sure enough, George!"

"But, Pa, who did make it there? who did make it there?"

"It grew there by chance, I suppose, my son."

"By chance, Pa! O no! no! it never did grow there by chance, Pa. Indeed that it never did!"

"High! why not, my son?"

2*

" Why, Pa, did you ever see any body's name in a plant bed before ?"

" Well, but George, such a thing might happen, though you never saw it before.

" Yes, Pa; but I did never see the little plants grow up so as to make one single letter of my name before. Now, how could they grow up so as to make all the letters of my name ! and then standing one after another, to spell my name so exactly !—and all so neat and even too, at top and bottom ! ! O Pa, you must not say chance did all this. Indeed somebody did it; and I dare say now, Pa, you did it just to scare me, because I am your little boy."

His father smiled ; and said, " Well George, you have guessed right. I indeed did it ; but not to scare you, my son; but to learn you a great thing which I wish you to understand. I want, my son, to introduce you to your true Father."

" High, Pa, an't you my true father, that has loved me, and been so good to me always ?"

" Yes George, I am your father, as the world calls it : and I love you very dearly too. But yet with all my love for you, George, I am but a poor good-for-nothing sort of a father in comparison of one you have."

" Aye ! I know, well enough whom you mean, Pa. You mean God Almighty ; don't you ?"

" Yes, my son, I mean him indeed. He is your true Father, George."

" But, Pa, where is God Almighty ! I did never see him yet."

" True my son; but though you never saw him, yet he is always with you. You did not see me when ten days ago I made this little plant bed, where you see your name in such beautiful green letters : but though you did not see me here, yet you know I was here ! !"

" Yes, Pa, that I do. I know you was here."

" Well then, and as my son could not believe that

chance had made and put together so exactly the
letters of his name, (though only sixteen) then how
can he believe, that chance could have made and put
together all those millions and millions of things that
are now so exactly fitted to his good! That my son
may look at every thing around him, see! what fine
eyes he has got! and a little pug nose to smell the
sweet flowers! and pretty ears to hear sweet sounds!
and a lovely mouth for his bread and butter! and O,
the little ivory teeth to cut it for him! and the dear
little tongue to prattle with his father! and precious
little hands and fingers to hold his play-things! and
beautiful little feet for him to run about upon! and
when my little rogue of a son is tired with running
about, then the still night comes for him to lie down:
and his mother sings, and the little crickets chirp him
to sleep! and as soon as he has slept enough, and
jumps up fresh and strong as a little buck, there the
sweet golden light is ready for him! When he looks
down into the water, there he sees the beautiful silver
fishes for him! and up in the trees there are the
apples, and peaches, and thousands of sweet fruits
for him! and all, all around him, wherever my dear
boy looks, he sees every thing just to his wants and
wishes;—the bubbling springs with cool sweet water
for him to drink! and the wood to make him sparkling fires when he is cold! and beautiful horses for
him to ride! and strong oxen to work for him! and
the good cow to give him milk! and bees to make
sweet honey for his sweeter mouth! and the little
lambs, with snowy wool, for beautiful clothes for
him! Now, these and all the ten thousand thousand
other good things more than my son can ever think
of, and all so exactly fitted to his use and delight—
Now how could chance ever have done all this for
my little son? Oh George!—

He would have gone on: but George, who had
hung upon his father's words with looks and eyes of
all-devouring attention, here broke out—

"Oh, Pa, that's enough! that's enough! It can't be chance, indeed—it can't be chance, that made and gave me all these things."

"What was it then, do you think, my son?"

"Indeed, Pa, I don't know unless it was God Almighty!"

"Yes, George, he it was, my son, and nobody else."

"Well, but Pa, (continued George) does God Almighty give me every thing? Don't you give me some things, Pa?"

"I give you something indeed! Oh how can I give you any thing, George! I who have nothing on earth that I can call my own, no, not even the breath I draw!"

"High, Pa! is'nt that great big house your house, and this garden, and the horses yonder, and oxen, and sheep, and trees, and every thing, is'nt all yours, Pa?"

"Oh no! my son! no! why you make me shrink into nothing, George, when you talk of all these belonging to me, who can't even make a grain of sand! Oh, how could I, my son, have given life to those great oxen and horses, when I can't give life even to a fly?—no! for if the poorest fly were killed, it is not your father, George, nor all the men in the world, that could ever make him alive again!"

At this, George fell into a profound silence, while his pensive looks showed that his youthful soul was labouring with some idea never felt before. Perhaps it was at that moment, that the good Spirit of God ingrafted on his heart that germ of piety, which filled his after life with so many of the precious fruits of morality.

CHAPTER III.

George's father dies—his education continued by his mother—his
behaviour under school-master Williams.

Thus pleasantly, on wings of down, passed away
the few short years of little George's and his father's
earthly acquaintance. Sweetly ruled by the sceptre of
reason, George almost adored his father; and thus
sweetly obeyed with all the cheerfulness of love, his
father doated on George. And though very different
in their years, yet parental and filial love rendered
them so mutually dear, that the old gentleman was
often heard to regret, that the school took his little
companion so much from him—while George, on the
other hand, would often quit his playmates to run
home and converse with his more beloved father.

But George was not long to enjoy the pleasure or
the profit of such a companion; for scarcely had he
attained his tenth year, before his father was seized
with the gout in his stomach, which carried him off
in a few days. George was not at home when his
father was taken ill. He was on a visit to some of his
cousins in Chotank, about twenty miles off: and his
father, unwilling to interrupt his pleasures, (for it was
but seldom that he visited) would not at first allow
him to be sent for. But finding that he was going
very fast, he begged that they would send for him in
all haste. He often asked if he was come; and said
how happy he should be once more to see his little
son, and give him his blessing before he died. But
alas! he never enjoyed that last mournful pleasure;
for George did not reach home until a few hours
before his father's death: and then he was speechless!
The moment he alighted, he ran into the chamber
where he lay. But oh! what were his feelings
when he saw the sad change that had passed upon
him! when he beheld those eyes, late so bright and

fond, now reft of all their lustre, faintly looking on
him from their hollow sockets, and through swelling
tears, in mute but melting language, bidding him a
last, last farewell!——Rushing with sobs and cries,
he fell upon his father's neck——he kissed him a
thousand and a thousand times, and bathed his clay-
cold face with scalding tears.

O happiest youth! Happiest in that love, which
thus, to its enamoured soul strained an aged, an
expiring sire. O! worthiest to be the founder of a
just and equal government lasting as thy own deathless name! And O! happiest old man! thus luxu-
riously expiring in the arms of such a child! O! well
requited for teaching him that love of his God (the
only fountain of every virtuous love) in return for
which he gave thee ('twas all he had) himself—his
fondest company—his sweetest looks and prattle.
He now gives thee his little feeble embraces. With
artless sighs and tears, faithful to thee still, his feet
will follow thee to thy grave: and when thy beloved
corse is let down to the stones of the pit, with streaming eyes he will rush to the brink, to take one more
look, while his bursting heart will give thee its last
trembling cry——O my father! my father!

But, though he had lost his best of friends, yet he
never lost those divine sentiments which that friend
had so carefully inculcated. On the contrary, interwoven with the fibres of his heart, they seemed to
" grow with his growth, and to strengthen with his
strength." The memory of his father, often bathed
with a tear—the memory of his father, now sleeping
in his grave, was felt to impose a more sacred obligation to do whatever he knew would rejoice his
departed shade. This was very happily displayed,
in every part of his deportment, from the moment of
his earliest intercourse with mankind.

Soon after the death of his father, his mother sent
him down to Westmoreland, the place of his nativity,
where he lived with his half-brother Augustine, and

went to school to a Mr. Williams, an excellent teacher in that neighbourhood. He carried with him his virtues, his zeal for unblemished character, his love of truth, and detestation of whatever was false and base. A gilt chariot with richest robes and liveried servants, could not half so substantially have befriended him; for in a very short time, so completely had his virtues secured the love and confidence of the boys, his word was just as current among them as a law. A very aged gentleman, formerly a school mate of his, has often assured me, (while pleasing recollection brightened his furrowed cheeks,) that nothing was more common, when the boys were in high dispute about a question of fact, than for some little shaver among the mimic heroes, to call out, "well boys! George Washington was there; Goorge Washington was there. He knows all about it: and if he don't say it was so, then we will give it up."—"Done," said the adverse party. Then away they would trot to hunt for George. Soon as his verdict was heard, the party favoured would begin to crow, and then all hands would return to play again.

About five years after the death of his father, he quitted school for ever, leaving the boys in tears for his departure: for he had ever lived among them, in the spirit of a brother. He was never guilty of so brutish a practice as that of fighting himself; nor would he, when able to prevent it, allow them to fight one another. If he could not disarm their savage passions by his arguments, he would instantly go to the master, and inform him of their barbarous intentions.

"The boys," said the same good old gentleman, "were often angry with George for this."—But he used to say, "angry or not angry, you shall never, boys, have my consent to a practice so shocking! shocking even in slaves and dogs; then how utterly scandalous in little boys at school, who ought to look on one another as brothers. And what must be the feelings of our tender parents, when, instead of seeing us come home smiling and lovely, as the joy of their hearts! they see us creeping in like young blackguards, with our heads bound up, black eyes, and bloody clothes! And what is all this for? Why, that we may get praise!! But the truth is, a quarrelsome boy was never sincerely praised! Big boys, of the vulgar sort, indeed may praise him: but it is only as they would a silly game cock, that fights for their pastime: and the little boys are sure to praise him, but it is only as they would a bull dog—to keep him from tearing them!!"

Some of his historians have said, and many believe, that Washington was a Latin scholar! But 'tis an error. He never learned a syllable of Latin. His second and last teacher, Mr. Williams, was indeed a capital hand—but not at Latin; for of that he understood perhaps as little as Balaam's ass. But at reading, spelling, English grammar, arithmetic, surveying, book keeping, and geography, he was indeed famous. And in these useful arts, 'tis said he often boasted that he had made young George Washington as great a scholar as himself.

Born to be a soldier, Washington early discovered symptoms of nature's intentions towards him. In his 11th year, while at school under old Mr. Hobby, he used to divide his play-mates into two parties or armies. One of these, for distinction sake, was called French, the other American. A big boy at the school, named William Bustle, commanded the former; George commanded the latter. And every day, at play-time, with corn-stalks for muskets, and calabashes for drums, the two armies would turn out, and march, and counter-march, and file off or fight their mimic battles, with great fury. This was fine sport for George, whose passion for active exercise was so strong, that at play-time no weather could keep him within doors. His fair cousins, who visited at his mother's, used to complain, that "George was not

fond of their company, like other boys; but soon as
ne had got his task, would run out to play." But
such trifling play as marbles and tops he could never
endure. They did not afford him exercise enough.
His delight was in that of the manliest sort, which,
by stringing the limbs and swelling the muscles,
promotes the kindliest flow of blood and spirits. At
jumping with a long pole, or heaving heavy weights,
for his years he hardly had an equal. And as to
running, the swift-footed Achilles could scarcely have
matched his speed.

"Egad! he ran wonderfully," said my amiable
and aged frieud, John Fitzhugh, Esq., who knew him
well. "We had nobody here-abouts, that could come
near him. There was a young Langhorn Dade, of
Westmoreland, a confounded clean made, tight young
fellow, and a mighty swift runner too. But then he
was no match for George. Langy, indeed, did not
like to give it up; and would brag that he had sometimes brought George to a tie. But I believe he was
mistaken: for I have seen them run together many a
time; and George always beat him easy enough."

Col. Lewis Willis, his play-mate and kinsman, has
been heard to say, that he has often seen him throw
a stone across Rappahannock, at the lower ferry of
Fredericksburg. It would be no easy matter matter
to find a man, now a-days, who could do it.

Indeed his father before him was a man of extraordinary strength. His gun, which to this day is
called Washington's fowling-piece, and is now the
property of Mr. Harry Fitzhugh, of Chotank, is of
such enormous weight, that not one man in fifty can
fire it without a rest. And yet throughout that country it is said, that he made nothing of holding it off
at arms length, and blazing away at the swans on
Potomac; of which he has been known to kill, rank
and file seven or eight at a shot.

But to return to George. It appears that from the
start he was a boy of an uncommonly warm and

3

noble heart; insomuch that Lawrence, though but his half-brother, took such a liking to him, even above his own brother Augustine, that he would always have George with him when he could; and often pressed him to come and live with him. But, as if led by some secret impulse, George declined the offer, and as we have seen, went to work in the back woods, as Lord Fairfax's surveyor! However, when Lawrence was taken with the consumption, and advised by his physicians to make a trip to Bermuda, George could not resist any longer, but hastened down to his brother at Mount Vernon, and went with him to Bermuda. It was at Bermuda that George took the small-pox, which marked him rather agreeably than otherwise. Lawrence never recovered, but returned to Virginia, where he died just after his brother George had fought his hard battle against the French and Indians, at Fort Necessity, as the reader will presently learn.

Lawrence did not live to see George after that; but he lived to hear of his fame; for as the French and Indians were at that time a great public terror, the people could not help being very loud in their praise of a youth, who, with so slender a force had dared to meet them in their own country, and had given them such a check.

And when Lawrence heard of his favorite young brother, that he had fought so gallantly for his country, and that the whole land was filled with his praise, he wept for joy. And such is the victory of love over nature, that though fast sinking under the fever and cough of a consumption in its extreme stage, he did not seem to mind it, but spent his last moments in fondly talking of his brother George, who, he said, " he had always believed, would one day or other be a great man!"

On openi g his will, it was found that George had lost nothing by his dutiful and affectionate behaviour to his brother Lawrence. For having now no issue, (his only child, a little daughter, lately dying) he left to George all his rich lands in Berkley, together with his great estate on Potomac, called MOUNT VERNON, in honour of old Admiral Vernon, by whom he had been treated with great politeness, while a volunteer with him at the unfortunate siege of Carthagena, in 1741.

CHAPTER IV.

George leaves school—is appointed a private surveyor to Lord Fairfax, of the Northern Neck—wishes to enter on board of a British man of war—providentially prevented by his mother—the first lightnings of his soul to war.

HAPPILY for America, George Washington was not born with "a silver spoon in his mouth." The Rappahannock plantatation left him by his father, was only in reversion—and his mother was still in her prime. Seeing then no chance of ever rising in the world but by his own merit, on leaving school he went up to Fairfax to see his brother Lawrence; with whom he found Mr. William Fairfax, one of the governor's council, who was come up on a visit to his sister, whom Lawrence had married. The counsellor presently took a great liking to George; and hearing him express a wish to get employment as a surveyor, introduced him to his relative, lord Fairfax, the wealthy proprietor of all those lands generally called the Northern Neck, lying between the Potomac and Rappahannock, and extending from Smith's Point on the Chesapeake, to the foot of the Great Allegheny. At the instance of the counsellor, Lord Fairfax readily engaged George as a surveyor; and sent him up into the back-woods to work. He continued in hs lordship's service till his 20th year, closely pursuing the laborious life of a woodsman.

From the manner in which Washington chose to

amuse his leisure hours during this period, I am almost inclined to think that he had a presentiment of the great labours that lay before him. When in Frederick, which at that time was very large, containing the counties now called Berkley, Jefferson, and Shenandoah, he boarded in the house of the widow Stevenson, generally pronounced Stinson. This lady had seven sons—William and Valentine Crawford, by her first husband; and John, and Hugh, and Dick, and Jim, and Mark Stinson, by her last husband. These seven young men, in Herculean size and strength, were equal, perhaps, to any seven sons of any one mother in Christendom. This was a family exactly to George's mind, because promising him an abundance of that manly exercise in which he delighted. In front of the house lay a fine extended green, with a square of several hundred yards. Here it was every evening, when his daily toils of surveying were ended, that George, like a young Greek training for the Olympic games, used to turn out with his sturdy young companions, " to see," as they termed it, " which was the best man," at running, jumping, and wrestling. And so keen was their passion for these sports, and so great their ambition to excel each other, that they would often persist, especially on moon-shining nights, till bedtime. The Crawfords and Stinsons, though not taller than George, were much heavier men; so that at wrestling, and particularly at the close or Indian hug, he seldom gained much matter of triumph. But in all trials of agility, they stood no chance with him!

From these Frederick county gymnastics or exercises, there followed an effect which shews the very wide difference between participating in innocent and guilty pleasures. While companions in raking and gambling, heartily despise and hate one another, and when they meet in the streets, pass each other with looks as cold and shy as sheep-thieving curs— these virtuous young men, by spending their even-

ings together, in innocent and manly exercises, con-
tracted a friendship which lasted for life.   When
George, twenty-five years after this, was called to
lead the American armies, he did not forget his old
friends, the Stinsons and Crawfords; but gave com-
missions to all of them who chose to join his army;
which several of them did.   William Crawford, the
eldest of them, and as brave a man as ever shouldered a musket, was advanced as high as the rank of
colonel, when he was burnt to death by the Indians
at Sandusky.   And equally cordial was the love of
these young men towards George, of whom they
always spoke as of a brother.   Indeed, Hugh Stinson, the second brother, who had a way of snapping
his eyes when he talked of any thing that greatly
pleased him, used to brighten up at the name of
Washington; and would tell his friends, that, " he
and his brother John had often laid the conqueror of
England on his back;" but at the same time, would
agree, that, " in running and jumping they were no
match for him."

Such was the way in which George spent his
leisure hours in the service of Lord Fairfax.   Little
did the old gentleman expect that he was educating
a youth, who should one day dismember the British
empire and break his own heart—which truly came
to pass.   For on hearing that Washington had captured Cornwallis and all his army, he called out to
his black waiter, " Come, Joe! carry me to my bed!
for I'm sure 'tis high time for me to die!"

> Then up rose Joe, all at the word
>   And took his master's arm,
> And to his bed he softly led,
>   The lord of Green-way farm.
>
> There he call'd on Britain's name
>   " And oft he wept full sore."—
> Then sigh'd—thy will, O Lord be done—.
>   " And word spake never more."

It was in his 15th year, according to the best of my information, that Washington first felt the kindlings of his soul for war. The cause was this—In those days the people of Virginia looked on Great Britain as the mother country; and to go thither was, in common phrase, "to go home." The name of OLD ENGLAND was music in their ears: and the bare mention of a blow meditated against her, never failed to rouse a something at the heart, which instantly flamed on the cheek, and flashed in the eye. Washington had his full share of these virtuous feelings: on hearing, therefore, that France and Spain were mustering a black cloud over his MOTHER COUNTRY, his youthful blood took fire; and he instantly tendered what aid his little arm could afford. The rank of midshipman was procured for him on board a British ship of war, then lying in our waters; and his trunk and clothes were actually sent on board. But when he came to take leave of his mother, she wept bitterly, and told him, she felt that her heart would break if he left her. George immediately got his trunk ashore! as he could not, for a moment, bear the idea of inflicting a wound on that dear life which had so long and so fondly sustained his own.

Where George got his great military talents, is a question which none but the happy believers in a particular Providence can solve: certain it is, his earthly parents had no hand in it. For of his father, tradition says nothing, save that he was a most amiable old gentlemen; one who made good crops, and scorned to give his name to the quill-drivers of a counting-room. And as to his mother, it is well known that she was none of Bellona's fiery race. For as some of the Virginia officers, just after the splendid actions of Trenton and Princeton, were complimenting her on the generalship and rising glory of her son, instead of shewing the exultation of a Spartan dame, she replied, with all the sang froid of a good old Friend, " Ah, dear me ! This fighting and killing is a sad thing ! I wish George would come home and look after his plantation ! !

Nor does it appear that nature had mixed much of gunpowder in the composition of any of his brothers; for when one of them, in the time of Braddock's war, wrote him a letter, signifying something like a wish to enter into the service; George, it is said, gave him this short reply : " Brother, stay at home, and comfort your wife."

But though not destined to figure on the quarterdeck of a man of war, yet he ceased not to cultivate that talent which had been given for higher uses. From adjutant Muse, a Westmoreland volunteer, who had gained much credit in the war of Cuba, whence he had lately returned with Lawrence Washington, he learnt to go through the manual exercise with great dexterity. By the help of good treatises on the art of war, which were put into his hands by the same gentleman, he soon acquired very clear ideas of the evolutions and movements of troops. And from Mons. Vanbraam, who afterwards accompanied him as interpreter to Venango, he acquired the art of fencing, at which, it is said, he was extremely expert. A passion, so uncommon for war, joined to a very manly appearance, and great dignity of character, could scarcely fail to attract on him the attention of the public. In fact the public sentiment was so strong in his favour, that at the green age of nineteen, he was appointed major and adjutant general of the Virginia forces in the Northern Neck, when training, as was expected, for immediate service.

For his services as an adjutant general, he was allowed by the crown one hundred pounds sterling per annum.

CHAPTER V.

French encroachments on the Ohio—Washington volunteers his service to governor Dinwiddie—his hazardous embassy to the French and Indians—miraculous escapes—account of his journal—anecdote of his modesty.

IN the year 1753 the people of Virginia were alarmed by a report that the French, aided by the Indians, were erecting a long line of military posts on the Ohio. This manœuvre, predicting no good to the ancient dominion, was properly resented by Robert Dinwiddie, the governor, who wished immediately in the name of his king to forbid the measure. But how to convey a letter to the French commandant on the Ohio, was the question. For the whole country west of the Blue Mountains, was one immeasurable forest, from time immemorial the gloomy haunt of ravening beasts and of murderous savages. No voices had ever broke the awful silence of those dreary woods, save the hiss of rattlesnakes, the shrieks of panthers, the yell of Indians, and howling tempests. From such scenes, though beheld but by the distant eye of fancy, the hearts of youth are apt to shrink with terror, and to crouch more closely to their safer fire-sides. But in the firmer nerves of Washington, they do not appear to have made the least impression of the agueish sort. The moment he heard of the governor's wishes, he waited on him with—a tender of his services.

"Now Christ save my saoul, but ye'er a braw lad !" said the good old Scotchman, " and gin ye play your cards weel, my boy, ye shall hae nae cause to rue your bargain." The governor took him to his palace that night, which was spent in preparing his letters and instructions. The next day, accompanied by an interpreter and a couple of servants, he set out on his journey, which, being in the depth of winter, was as disagreeable and dangerous as Hercules himself could have desired. Drenching rains and drowning floods, and snow-covered mountains opposed his course; but opposed in vain. The generous ambition to serve his country, and to distinguish himself, carried him through all; and, even at the most trying times, touched his heart with a joy unknown to the vain and trifling. On his way home he was way-laid and shot at by an Indian, who, though not fifteen paces distant, happily missed his aim. The poor wretch was made prisoner. But Washington could not find in his heart to put him to death, though his own safety seemed to require the sacrifice. The next evening, in attempting to cross a river on a raft, he was within an ace of being drowned; and, the night following, of perishing in the ice; but from both these imminent deadly risks, there was a hand unseen that effected his escape.

About the middle of January he returned to Williamsburgh; and, instantly waiting on the governor, presented him the fruits of his labours—the belts of wampum which he had brought from the Indian kings as pledges of their friendship—the French governor's letters—and, last of all, his journal of the expedition. This, it seems, he had drawn up as a tub for the whale, that he might be spared the pain of much talking about himself and his adventures. For like the king of Morven, " though mighty deeds rolled from his soul of fire, yet his words were never heard.' The governor was much pleased with the Indian belts —more with the Frenchman's letter—but most of all with Washington's journal, which he proposed to have printed immediately. Washington begged that his excellency would spare him the mortification of seeing his journal sent out into the world in so mean a dress. He urged, that having been written in a wintry wilderness, by a traveller, young, illiterate, and often cold, wet, and weary, it needed a thousand amendments. " Hoot awa, Major," replied his excellency, "hoot awa, mon; what tauk ye aboot amendments. I am sure the pamphlet need nae blush to be seen by his majesty himsel—and in geud troth I mean to send him a copy or twa of it. And besides our Assembly will rise to-morrow or next day, and I wish each of the members to tak a few copies hame with them. So we must e'en strait-way print the journal off hand as it is."

The journal, of course, was immediately printed. Every eye perused it: and every tongue was loud in its praise. Indeed it was not easy to err on the side of excess; for whoever with candour reads the journal, will readily pronounce it an unique in the history of juvenile productions. It discovers that vigour, and variety of talents, which take up, as it were intuitively, the views belonging to any new subject that presents itself. It is the hasty production of a young man, born in retreats of deepest solitude, in a time of profoundest peace, and brought up to the simple harmless employment of a surveyor, an employment which, more than any other, tends to tranquillize the mind. The verdure and music of the love-breathing spring; the bright fields and harvests of joy-inspiring summer; the faded leaves and mournful silence of autumn, with winter's solemn grandeur; were the scenes in which the youth of Washington was passed. In these he hears the roar of distant war—from these he is sent forth to mark the gathering storm. Instantly he breathes the whole spirit of his new engagement—"Old things are done away: all things are become new." The chain and theodolite are forgotten—the surveyor is lost in the soldier. His shoulders are young: but they sustain the head of an old engineer. He marks the soil, the timber, the confluence of rivers, the sites for forts. In short, nothing connected with the defence of his country escapes him. He penetrates the characters of the different people around him—the low sensuality of the Indian, ready, for a dram, to lift the tomahawk—

the polished subtleties of the European, who can
" smile and smile," and yet design the death of the
traveller. These important truths present themselves
intuitively to his mind; and shine with such lustre in
the pages of his journal, as to command the admiration of every unprejudiced reader.

Among the gentlemen in Williamsburgh, who had
sense and virtue enough to appreciate the worth of
Washington, one of the first was a Mr. Waller.
This gentleman, conversing on that subject with Mr.
Robertson, speaker of the house of Burgesses, observed, that such services as those rendered by Major
Washington, were far too important to be paid off by
the light coin of common parlour puffs. " This young
man," said he, " has deserved well of his country;
and her Representatives in Assembly ought to acknowledge the obligation." That's exactly my own
opinion," replied Robertson : " and if you will let me
know when the major next visits us, I will make a
motion to that effect."

The next day, Washington, not having ever dreamt
of the honour intended him, entered the house; and,
going up stairs, took his seat in the gallery.   The
eagle-eyed friendship of Mr. Waller quickly discovered him; and stepping to the chair, whispered it to
Mr. Robertson; who instantly arose, and ordering
silence, called out : " Gentlemen, it is proposed that
the thanks of this house be given to Major Washington, who now sits in the gallery, for the very gallant
manner in which he executed the important trust
lately reposed in him by his excellency governor
Dinwiddie."   In a moment the house rose as one
man; and turning towards Washington, saluted him
with a general bow; and, in very flattering terms,
expressed their high sense of his services.   Had an
earthquake shaken the capitol to the centre, it could
hardly have so completely confounded the major!
He rose to make his acknowledgments, but, alas; his
tongue had forgotten its office. Thrice he essayed to

speak: but thrice, in spite of every effort, his utterance failed him, save faintly to articulate, " Mr. Speaker, Mr. Speaker!" To relieve him from his embarrassment, Mr. Robertson kindly called out, " Major Washington, Major Washington, sit down; your modesty alone is equal to your merit."

CHAPTER VI.

The French and Indian war begins—Washington goes forth to meet the dangers of his country—aims a blow at Fort Du Quesne—fails —gallant defence of Fort Necessity—retires from the service in disgust—pressed into it again by General Braddock—defeat and death of Braddock, and dreadful slaughter of his army.

"WELL, what is to come, will come!" said poor Paddy, when going to the gallows. Even so was come, as would seem, the time that was to come for " kings to go forth to battle." The truth is, numbers of poor tax-ground, and thence uneducated and half-starved wretches in Britain and France, were become diseased with a mortal cachexy or surcharge of bad humours; such as gambling, swindling, horse stealing, highway robbing, &c. which nothing but the saturnine pills and steel points of Mars could effectually carry off. Thus in all corrupted governments war is considered as a necessary evil. It was no doubt necessary then.

Such was the remote cause. The proximate history, or how the dance begun, we now proceed to relate.

We have just seen that the French, pouring down from the lakes of Canada, thick as autumnal geese, were dashing away on the Ohio, at an alarming rate —multiplying forts—holding talks—and strengthening their alliances with the Indians. And we have seen, that Washington, with letters from governor Dinwiddie, had been out among the parlezvous, conjuring them by every thing venerable in treaties, or valuable in peace, to desist from such unwarrantable measures. But all to no purpose: for the French commandant, smiling at Washington, as a green horn, and at Dinwiddie as an old fool, continued his operations as vigorously as though he knew not that the country in question made a part of the British empire.

Swift as the broad-winged packets could fly across the deep, the news was carried to England. Its effect there was like that of a stone rudely hurled against a nest of hornets. Instantly, from centre to circumference, all is rage and bustle—the hive resounds with the maddening insects. Dark tumbling from their cells they spread the hasty wing, and shrill whizzing through the air, they rush to find the foe. Just so in the sea-ruling island, from queens house to ale-house, from king to cockney, all were fierce for fight. Even the red-nosed porters where they met, bending under their burdens, would stop in the streets, to talk of England's wrong: and, as they talked, their fiery snouts were seen to grow more fiery still, and more deformed. Then throwing their packs to the ground, and leaping into the attitude of boxers, with sturdy arms across, and rough black jaws stretched out, they bend forward to the fancied fight! The frog-eating foe, in shirtless ruffles and long lank queue seems to give ground! then rising in their might, with fire-striking eyes they press hard upon him; and coming in, hand and foot, with kick and cuff, and many a hearty curse, they show the giggling crowd, how, damn 'em, they would thump the French.

The news was brought to Britain's king just as he had dispatched his pudding; and sat, right royally amusing himself with a slice of Gloucester and a nip of ale. From the lips of the king down fell the luckless cheese, alas! not grac'd to comfort the stomach of the Lord's anointed; while, crowned

4

with, snowy foam, his nut-brown ale stood untasted beside his plate. Suddenly as he heard the news, the monarch darkened in his place; and answering darkness shrouded all his court.

In silence he rolled his eyes of fire on the floor, and twirled his terrible thumbs! his pages shrunk from his presence; for who could stand before the king of thundering ships, when wrath, in gleams of lightning, flashed from his "dark red eyes?" Starting at length, as from a trance, he swallowed his ale: then clenching his fist, he gave the table a tremendous knock, and cursed the wooden-shoed nation by his God! Swift as he cursed, the dogs of war bounded from their kennels, keen for the chase: and, snuffing the blood of Frenchmen on every gale, they raised a howl of death which reached these peaceful shores. Orders were immediately issued, by the British government, for the colonies to arm and unite in one confederacy. Virginia took the lead; and raised a regiment, to the second command in which she raised her favourite Washington. Colonel Fry, by right of seniority, commanded : but on his death, which happened soon after his appointment, Washington succeeded to the command. With this little handful, he bravely pushed out into the wilderness, in quest of the enemy; and at a place called the Little Meadows, came up with a party under one Jumonville. This officer was killed, and all his men taken prisoners.

From these prisoners, he obtained undoubted intelligence, that the French troops on the Ohio, consisted of upwards of a thousand regulars, and many hundreds of Indians. But notwithstanding this disheartening intelligence, he still pressed on undauntedly against the enemy, and, at a place called the Great Meadows, built a fort, which he called Fort Necessity.

Soon as the lines of the entrenchments were marked off, and the men about to fall to work, Washington seizing the hand of the first that was lifting the spade, cried out "Stop, my brave fellow! my hand must heave the first earth that is thrown up in defence of this country!"

Leaving a small garrison behind him, he dashed on for Fort Duquesne, (Fort Pitt,) hoping by the reduction of that important post, to strike terror into the enemy, and defeat their plans. But though this was a bold stroke of generalship, yet it appeared that he had not a force, sufficient to effect it. For in the midst of this day's march, he was met by a party of friendly Indians, who, running up to him, with looks and gestures greatly agitated, cried out: "Fly! fly! don't look behind you! your enemies are upon you, thick as the pigeons in the woods!"

Washington called a council of his officers, who advised an immediate return to Fort Necessity, which they hardly recovered before their sentinels fired an alarm; came running in; and stated that the woods were alive with Frenchmen and Indians! It should have been observed, that the dreadful news of the day before, had produced so shameful a desertion among his troops in the course of the night, that when the enemy attacked, which they did with 1500 men, Washington had but 300 to stand by him. But never did the true Virginia valour shine more gloriously than on this trying occasion,—to see 300 young fellows—commanded by a smooth-faced boy —all unaccustomed to the terrors of war—far from home—and from all hope of help—shut up in a dreary wilderness—and surrounded by five times their number of savage foes, yet without sign of fear, preparing for mortal combat! Scarcely since the days of Leonidas and his three hundred deathless Spartans, had the sun beheld its equal. With hideous whoops and yells, the enemy came on like a host of tigers. The woods and rocks, and tall tree-tops, filled with Indians, were in one continued blaze and crash of fire-arms. Nor were our youthful warriors idle: but animated by their youthful commander, they plied their rifles with such spirit, that the little fort resembled a volcano in full blast, roaring and discharging thick sheets of liquid fire and of leaden deaths among their foes. For nine glorious hours, salamander-like, enveloped in smoke and flames, they sustained the attack of the enemy's whole force, and laid two hundred of them dead on the spot! Discouraged by such desperate resistance, the French general, the Count de Villiers, sent in a flag to Washington, highly extolling his gallantry, and offering him the most honourable terms. It was stipulated, that Washington and his little band of heroes, should march away with all the honours of war, and carry with them their military stores and baggage.

On their return to the bosom of their country, they were every where received with the praises which they had so well deserved. The Legislature voted the thanks of the nation to Washington and his officers; with a pistole to each of his men, about 300.

In the course of the following winter, notice was given from the mother country, that American officers, acting with the British, should bear no command!! Hence the poorest shoat, if wearing the proud epaulette of a Briton, might command a Wolfe, if so unlucky as to be an American!!! Incensed at such an outrage on common justice, and the rights of his countrymen, Washington threw up his commission, and retired to his plantation, Mount Vernon, lately left him by his brother Lawrence. Here, Cincinnatus-like, he betook him to his favorite plough. But the season called for the sword; and he was now risen too high to be overlooked in times like those when troubles and fears began to darken over all the land.

The report of his gallant but unsuccessful struggle with the French and Indians, soon reached England: and the ministry thinking the colonies alone too weak to repel the enemy, hurried on General Braddock, with two heavy regiments, to their aid. This reinforcement arrived early in the spring of 1755. Leaving them at the Capes on their way up to Belle-haven, (now Alexandria,) Braddock called at Williamsburgh, to see Governor Dinwiddie, who attended him to Alexandria.

"Where is Colonel Washington?" said General Braddock. "I long to see him."

"He is retired from the service, Sir," replied the Governor.

"Retired! Sir!" continued the General, "Colonel Washington retired! pray, Sir, what's the reason?"

On hearing the cause, he broke into a passion against the order from the war-office as a shameful piece of partiality—and extolled Colonel Washington as "a young man of sense and spirit, who knew and asserted his rights as became a soldier and a British subject."

He then wrote to Washington, whom he pressingly invited to join his army, and accept the rank of a volunteer aid-de-camp in his own family. This invitation was cheerfully accepted by our young countryman, who waited on General Braddock as soon as he heard of his arrival at Alexandria. About the same time, three companies of excellent Virginia marksmen, raised by order of the Legislature, arrived at the British camp.

It was in the month of June, 1755, that the army, upwards of 2000 strong, left Alexandria; and, with their faces to the west, began their march to the mournful ditty of "over the hills and far away." On the route Washington was taken sick; and by the time they had reached the Little Meadows, had become so very ill, that Braddock, at the instance of the physicians, insisted most peremptorily that he should lie by until Colonel Dunbar with the rear of the army came up. With great reluctance he yielded to their wishes. But so great were his fears for the army, lest in those wild woods it should fall into some Indian snare, that the moment his fever left

him, he mounted his horse, and pursued, and overtook them the very evening before they fell into that
ambuscade which he had all along dreaded. For
the next morning, the 9th of July, when they were
safely arrived within seven miles of Fort Duquesne!
and so confident of success, that their general swore
he would that night sup either in Fort Duquesne or
in the lower regions—behold, the Virginia Rangers
discovered signs of Indians.

Here Washington, with his usual modesty, observed to General Braddock what sort of an enemy he
had now to deal with—an enemy who would not,
like the Europeans, come forward to a fair contest in
the field, but concealed behind the rocks and trees,
carry on a deadly warfare with their rifles. He
concluded with these words, "I beg of your excellency the honour to allow me to lead on with the
Virginia Riflemen, and fight them in their own way."

Had it been decreed that this hapless army should
have been saved, this was the counsel to have effected
it. But it would seem, alas! that heaven had
ordained their fall in that distant land; and there
with their flesh to fatten the wolves and vultures on
the hills of Monongahela. For General Braddock,
who had all along treated the American officers with
infinite contempt, rejected Washington's counsel, and
swelling with most unmanly rage, replied, " High
times, by —— High times! when a young Buckskin
can teach a British General how to fight!" Instantly
the pale, fever-worn cheeks of Washington turned
fiery red. But smothering his feelings, he rode
towards his men, biting his lips with grief and rage,
to think how many brave fellows would draw short
breath that day through the pride and obstinacy of
one epauletted madman. Formed in heavy columns
the troops continued to advance. A little beyond
the Monongahela, was a narrow defile, through which
lay their road, with moss-grown rocks on either side,
and aged trees that spread an awful shade. Here,
in perfect concealment, the French and Indians lay,

waiting impatiently for this devoted army. Too
soon, alas! the army came up, and entering the defile,
moved along in silence, like sheep to the slaughter,
little dreaming how close the bloody fates hovered
around them. Thinking their prey now completely
in their clutches, all at once, the Indians set up the
most hideous yells, as if the woods were filled with
ten thousand panthers. This they did, both as a
terror to the British, and a signal to attack; for in
the same moment they poured in a general fire, which
instantly covered the ground with death in every
hideous shape. Some were seen sinking pale and
lifeless at once, giving up the ghost with only a
hollow groan—others rolling on the earth, convulsed
and shrieking in the last agonies, while life and life's
warm blood together gushed in hissing torrents from
their breasts. Such sights of their bleeding comrades,
had the enemy but been in view, instead of depress-
ing would but have inflamed British blood with
fiercer thirst for vengeance. But, alas! to be thus
entrapped in a dreary wild! to be thus pent up, and
shot from behind rocks and trees, by an invisible
enemy, was enough to dismay the stoutest hearts.
Their native valour, however, and confidence in
themselves, did not at once forsake them. But,
animated by their officers, they stood their ground,
and for a considerable time fought like heroes. But
seeing no impression made by their fire, while that
of the enemy, heavy as at first, with fatal flashes
continued to cut down their ranks, they at length
took a panic, and fell into great confusion. Happily,
on the left, where lay the deadliest fire, Washington's
rangers were posted; but not exposed like the
British. For, on hearing the horrible savage yells,
in a moment they flew each to his tree, like the
Indians; and like them, each levelled his rifle, and
with as deadly aim. This, through a kind Providence, saved Braddock's army; for exulting in their
confusion, the savages, grimly painted, yelling like
furies, burst from their coverts, eager to glut their

hellish rage with a total massacre of the British. But, faithful to their friends, Washington's rangers stepped forth with joy to meet the assailants. Then rose a scene sufficient to fill the stoutest heart with horror. Burning alike for vengeance, both parties throw aside the slow-murdering rifles, and grasp their swift-fated tomahawks. Dreadfully above their heads gleams the brandished steel, as with full exerted limbs, and faces all inflamed with mortal hate, they level at each other their last decisive blows. Death rages through all their fast-thinning ranks—his bleeding victims are rolled together on every side. Here falls the brave Virginia Blue, under the stroke of his nimbler foe—and there, man on man the Indians perish beneath the furious tomahawks, deep buried in the shattered brain. But who can tell the joy of Washington, when he saw this handful of his despised countrymen thus gallantly defending their British friends, and by dint of mortal steel driving back their blood thirsty assailants. Happy check! for by this time, covered with wounds Braddock had fallen—his aids and officers, to a man, killed or wounded—and his troops, in hopeless, helpless despair, flying backwards and forwards from the fire of the Indians, like flocks of crowding sheep from the presence of their butchers. Washington alone remained unhurt! Horse after horse had been killed under him. Showers of bullets had touched his locks or pierced his regimentals. But still protected by heaven—still supported by a strength not his own, he had continued to fly from quarter to quarter, where his presence was most needed, sometimes animating his rangers; sometimes striving, but in vain, to rally the regulars. 'Twas his lot to be close to the brave but imprudent Braddock when he fell; and he assisted to place him in a tumbril, or little cart. As he was laid down, pale and near spent, with loss of blood, he faintly said to Washington—

"Well, Colonel, what's to be done now?"

DEFEAT OF GENERAL BRADDOCK.

"Retreat, Sir," replied Washington: "retreat by all means; for the Regulars won't fight; and the Rangers are nearly all killed !"

"Poor fellows !" he replied, "poor fellows !—Well, do as you will, Colonel, do as you will."

The army then commenced its retreat, in a very rapid and disorderly manner, while Washington with his few surviving rangers, covered the rear.

Happily, the Indians did not pursue them far: but after firing a few random shots, returned in a body, to fall upon the plunder; while Washington, with his frightened fugitives continued their retreat, sadly remembering that more than one half of their morning's gay companions were left a prey to the ravening beasts of the desert. There, denied the common charities of the grave, they lay for many a year bleaching the lonely hills with their bones.

On reaching Fort Cumberland, where they met Colonel Dunbar with the rear of the army, General Braddock died. He died in the arms of Washington, whose pardon he often begged for having treated him so rudely that fatal morning—heartily wished, he said, he had but followed his advice—frequently called his rangers " brave fellows ! glorious fellows !" Often said, he should be glad to live if it was only to reward their gallantry ! I have more than once been told, but cannot vouch for the truth of it, that his sister, on hearing how obstinately Washington and his Blues had fought for her brother, was so affected that she shed tears: and sent them from England handsome cockades, according to their number, and a pair of colours elegantly wrought by her own fair hands.

With respect to Washington, I cannot but mention here two very extraordinary speeches that were made about him, after Braddock's defeat, and which, as things have turned out, look a good deal like prophecies. A famous Indian warrior, who acted a leading part in that bloody tragedy, was often heard to swear, that "Washington was never born to be killed by a bullet! For," continued he "I had seventeen fair fires at him with my rifle, and after all could not bring him to the ground!" And indeed whoever considers that a good rifle levelled by a proper marksman, hardly ever misses its aim, will readily enough conclude with this unlettered savage, that there was some invisible hand that turned aside the bullets.

The Rev. Mr. Davies, in a sermon occasioned by Braddock's defeat, has these remarkable words—"I beg leave to point the attention of the public to that heroic youth Colonel Washington, whom I cannot but hope Providence has preserved for some great service to this country!!"

But though the American writers have pretty unanimously agreed, that Washington was, under God, the saving Angel that stood up between Braddock's army and total destruction, yet did it profit him but little with his sovereign. The British officers indeed admired him: but they had no idea of going any farther: "To tell in Gath, or publish in the streets of Askalon" that a British army owed its safety to a young Buckskin, required a pitch of virtue and of courage above ordinary minds. Washington was therefore kept in the back ground; and General Braddock being dead, the command devolved upon Colonel Dunbar, whose conduct proved him to be one of those pusillanimous hirelings, who flee when the wolf cometh. To attempt, by some gallant effort to recover what Braddock had lost,—or to hang upon the enemy, and prevent, at least, those numerous scalping parties, which distracted with midnight murders and deluged the defenceless frontiers with blood, were brave and generous ideas, of which he seemed incapable. But, trembling under the general panic, he instantly ordered the tents to be struck; and pushing off under the whip and spur of his fears, never halted until he had reached Philadelphia; where he went, as he called it, into winter quarters, (in the beginning of the dog-days!) leaving all the frontiers of Maryland and Virginia exposed to the merciless tomahawk.

Such facts ought to be recorded for the benefit of young men, who, with no military qualifications but big limbs, can yet covet red coats and shoulder-knots.

Being thus shamefully deserted by Colonel Dunbar, Washington with his thirty rangers, set out with sorrowful hearts to return home. But before he left Fort Cumberland, he dispatched an express, to inform Governor Dinwiddie, that "General Braddock was slain—his army totally defeated—the remnant on their march to Philadelphia—and the whole frontier given up to the Indians!" The consternation that was spread throughout the country by this news, was inexpressible. Heart-sickening terrors, as of a woman in labour, seized upon all families——and a frightened fancy found food for its fears in every thing around it—the blast whistling round the corners of their cabin, alarmed, like the yell of murderous savages—the innocent death-bell—the croaking raven—the midnight howl of dogs——were all sure harbingers of fate. While, for dread of the Indians, the roads were filled with thousands of distracted parents, with their weeping little ones, flying from their homes.

The Governor instantly ordered a call of the Legislature, who, by the time Washington reached Williamsburgh, were assembled, and, together with numbers of citizens, went out and met him near the own.

The interview was tender. For the citizens were almost moved to tears, when they saw that of so many of their brave countrymen who went forth to battle, only this little handful remained! They were exceedingly rejoiced to see, alive, and well, their beloved Washington. He had always been dear to them; but now doubly dear, in such times of danger. They mourned the misfortunes of their country; but laid

5

no blame to him. On the contrary, it was universally believed, that, but for him the ruin would have been complete. " Braddock," said they, " lost the victory : but Washington saved the army."

CHAPTER VII.

Fatal effects of Braddock's defeat—Washington wishes to carry the war into the Indian country—government refuses—defensive war preferred—the frontiers desolated.

GREAT was the joy at Fort Duquesne on the return of their troops from the slaughter of Braddock's army. The idea of victory, as appeared afterwards, had never once entered their heads.—They had gone out just to reconnoitre, and harass the British in their approach! How unbounded then must have been the joy of the garrison, on seeing their friends come back next morning, not sad and spiritless, as had been expected, but whooping and shouting for a glorious victory; and enriched with the artillery, ammunition, provisions, and baggage-waggons of a British army cut to pieces!!

The French commandant took care to make a proper use of his advantage; for as soon as the days of savage feasting and drunkenness were over, he sent out deputations of his chiefs with grand-talks to several of the neighbouring tribes, who had not yet lifted the hatchet.

The tribes being assembled, and the calumet or pipe of friendship smoked around, the chiefs arose; and in all the pomp of Indian eloquence announced their great victory over Long Knife (the Virginians) and his white brothers, (the British)—then with a proud display of the numerous scalps and rich dresses which they had taken, they concluded with inviting

the young men to unbury the tomahawk, and rush
with them to drink the blood of their enemies.

This was enough—"Grinning horribly a ghastly
smile," at such prospects of blood and plunder, the
grim children of the desert, rose up at once to war.
No time was lost in preparation. A pouch of parched corn, and a bear-skin, with a rifle, tomahawk,
and scalping knife, were their equipage. And in a
few weeks after Braddock's defeat, an army of at
least fourteen hundred of those blood-thirsty savages
were in full march over hills and mountains, to surprise and murder the frontier inhabitants.

Washington had early foreseen the storm that
would one day burst from Fort Du Quesne. On his
first trip through that country, two years before, he
had marked the very spot, and pointed it out as "the
key of the western world." But Britain and America,
(like the wild ass and her colts, though mule-stubborn
in acting, yet snail-slow to act,) let the golden chance
escape; till one Du Quesne, a French officer, with
some troops, passing along that way in 1754, and
struck, as Washington had been, with the situation,
immediately built thereon a fort, which he called
after his own name. It answered the fatal purposes
which Washington had predicted. By means of the
bold water courses on which it stood, it greatly
favoured the conveyance both of goods and of intelligence. There the French laid up magazines for their
Indian allies, and there they hoisted the dread signals
of war.

Not having been able to prevail on his countrymen
to occupy it before the enemy, Washington's whole
ambition now was to take it from them. "Send two
thousand men,"—said he, in numerous importunate
letters to the Governor and Legislature, "send two
thousand men, and drain the fountain at once—the
streams will fail of course."

But, spite of this advice, the mad policy of a
defensive war prevailed in the Virginia Government:

and instead of raising 2000 men, they voted to raise about half that number! and then, like hypocrites who make up in lip-service what they lack in good works, they dubbed him Commander in chief of all the troops raised or to be raised in Virginia, with the privilege of naming his own field officers!

These vain honours served but to exalt him to a higher sphere of misery—the misery of taking a wider survey of those misfortunes of his country which he could not remedy,—and to feel a deeper responsibility for those blunders of others, which he could not cure. He saw Fort Duquesne mustering her murderers, which he had no powers to prevent! He had a frontier of 360 miles to defend, and generally less than 700 men to defend it with! If he kept his troops embodied, the whole country would be left open to the savages. If he broke them down into small parties, they might be destroyed one after another, by a superior force. If he threw them into forts, they were sure to be starved; or derided by the enemy, who could easily pass them in the night and surprise, destroy, and murder the inhabitants with impunity. And though thus completely crippled by the stupidity or parsimony of the government, and incapacitated from doing any services for his country, yet great services were expected of him, and great blame bestowed for every failure. If no victories were gained over the enemy, he would be blamed for inactivity. If the settlers were murdered, he would be accused of neglect—and if he pointed out the errors of government, he would be charged as "officious" and "impertinent;" and this while young officers of the worthless sort, mere cork-drawers and songsters at great men's tables, were basely cutting in with a weak old governor's prejudices, to work him out, and to worm themselves into favour and rank.

But all these vexations and sorrows were but trifles in comparison of others which he was doomed to feel. Seeing no hopes of a force sufficient to attack

Fort Duquesne, he formed a chain of garrisons along the frontier; and then, with a flying corps of the most active and daring young men, continued night and day, to scour the country in quest of the enemy's murdering parties. In this bold and dangerous employment, which lasted almost three years, he was often presented with sights of human destruction, sufficient to excite sympathy in hearts of flintiest stone.

On cautiously entering the hapless plantation with his men, they halt and listen awhile—but hear no voice of man—see no house, nor sign of habitation— all is void and silent. Marking the buzzards perched on the trees in the corn-fields, they approach, and find, lying by his plough, the half-devoured carcass of a man. The hole in his breast shows that he had been shot, while the deep gashes in the forehead of his dead horses, point out the bursting strokes of the tomahawk. Amidst the ashes of the late dwelling, are seen, white as chalk, the bones of the mother and her children. But sometimes their raw and bloody skeletons, fed on by the hogs, are found in the yards or gardens where they were surprised.

" One day"—said he to an intimate ; though it was but seldom that he mentioned those things, they gave nim so much pain—" One day, as we drew near through the woods, to a dwelling, suddenly we heard the discharge of a gun. Whereupon quickening our pace, and creeping up through the thick bushes to a fence, we saw what we had dreaded—a party of Indians, loaded with plunder, coming out of a house, which, by the smoke, appeared as if it were just set on fire. In a moment we gave the savages a shower of rifle balls, which killed every man of them but one. He attempted to run off. It was in vain. Some of our swift-footed hunters gave chase, and soon overtook and immolated him with their toma- hawks. On rushing into the house, and putting out the fire, we saw a mournful sight indeed—a young woman lying on a bed floating in blood—her fore-

5*

head cleft with a hatchet—and on her breast two
little children, apparently twins, and about nine
months old, bathing her bosom with the crimson
currents flowing from their deeply gashed heads! I
had often beheld the mangled remains of my murdered countrymen; but never before felt what I did
on this occasion. To see these poor innocents—
these little unoffending angels, just entered upon life,
and, instead of fondest sympathy and tenderness,
meeting their hideous deaths; and from hands of
brothers too! filled my soul with the deepest horror
of sin! but at the same time inspired a most adoring
sense of that religion which announces the Redeemer,
who shall, one day, do away man's malignant
passions, and restore the children of God to primeval
love and bliss. Without this hope, what man of feeling but would wish he had never been born!

On tracing back into the corn-field the steps of the
barbarians, we found a little boy, and beyond him
his father, both weltering in blood. It appeared,
from the print of his little feet in the furrows, that the
child had been following his father's plough; and,
seeing him shot down, had set off with all his might, to
get to the house to his mother; but was overtaken,
and destroyed!

"And, indeed, so great was the dread entertained
of the French and Indians, throughout the settlements, that it was distressing to call even on those
families who yet survived, but, from sickness or other
causes, had not been able to get away. The poor
creatures would run to meet us, like persons half
distracted with joy——and then with looks blank
with terror, would tell that such or such a neighbour's family, perhaps the very night before, was
murdered!—and that they heard their cries!—and
saw the flames that devoured their houses!—and
also, that they themselves, after saying their prayers
at night, never lay down to sleep, without first taking
leave of one another, as if they never expected to

meet again in this world. But when we came to take our leave of these wretched families, my God! what were our feelings! to see the deep, silent grief of the men; and the looks of the poor women and children, as, falling upon their knees, with piercing screams, and eyes wild with terror, they seized our hands, or hung to our clothes, intreating us, for God's sake, and for mercy sake, not to leave them. I remember, "These things so harrassed my heart with grief, that I solemnly declare to God, if I know myself, I would gladly offer my own life a sacrifice to the butchering enemy, if I could thereby insure the safety of these my poor distressed countrymen.

Such were the scenes in which Washington was doomed to spend three years of a wretched life, rendered still more wretched by knowing so perfectly as he did, that the rapid charge of two thousand brave fellows upon Fort Duquesne, like the thundering shock of a two-and-forty pounder upon a water-spout, would have instantly dispersed the fatal meteor, and restored the golden hours of peace and safety. But to give Colonel Washington two thousand men, seemed to old governor Dinwiddie, like giving the staff out of his own hand, as he elegantly called it; and rather than do that, he would risk the desolation of the western country, by continuing a defensive war, and a mad dependence on a disorderly militia, who would come and go as they pleased—get drunk and sleep when they pleased—whoop and halloo where they pleased—and, in short, serve no other purpose on earth but to disgrace their officers, deceive the settlers, and defraud the public. Indeed so ruinous were these measures of governors Dinwiddie and Loudon, that, in the short space of three years, they completely broke up all the fine young settlements to the westward of Winchester, Fredericktown, and Carlisle, whereby numbers of poor people were butchered! hundreds of rich plantations deserted! myriads of produce lost! and thousands of dollars

sunk! and all for the sake of saving the paltry
expense of raising in the first instance a force which
would in ten weeks have taken Fort Duquesne, and
completely broken up that den of thieves and murderers!

At length, in 1758, the government of Virginia
devolved on general Forbes, who, to the infinite
satisfaction of Washington, consented to second his
views on Fort Duquesne.   Washington earnestly
recommended an early campaign, lest the Indian
warriors who were to meet them in April at Winchester, should grow tired of waiting, and return home.
But the season was, unfortunately, so idled away,
that marching orders were not given till the first of
September, when, according to Washington's prediction, there was not a red man to be found in camp.
The army then commenced its movements, but still
as would seem, under the frown of heaven.

For instead of sweeping along the old track, generally called Braddock's road, Gen. Forbes was persuaded to take an entirely new route, of which every
inch was to be cut through wilds and mountains
covered with rocks and trees!   In vain Washington
remonstrated against this as a measure, "which" he
said, "if persisted in at this late season, would
certainly ruin the undertaking."—General Forbes
was inflexible.

In a letter to the Speaker of the House of Burgesses, Washington has these remarkable words—"If
this conduct of our leaders, do not flow from superior
orders, it must flow from a weakness, too gross for
me to name.   Nothing now but a miracle can bring
this campaign to a happy issue."   In a letter of a
later date he says, "well, all's lost! our enterprise is
ruined!   And we shall be stopped this winter at the
Laurel Hills!"

By the middle of November, after incredible exertions, the army, sure enough, reached the Laurel
Hills, where Washington predicted it would winter!

and strange to tell! General Forbes, with a caucus squad of his officers were actually in deep debate, whether they should spend the winter in that inhospitable wild, or tread back their mournful steps to Winchester, when some prisoners brought the welcome news that the garrison of Fort Duquesne, for a long time past unsupported by their countrymen, and now deserted by the Indians, was so reduced, that they would surrender at the sight of an enemy. General Forbes instantly changed his mind, and with a select detachment made a push for Fort Duquesne, the ruins of which he entered, without opposition, on the 28th of November, 1758. For, advertised of his approach, the French determined to quit it; and after having set fire to the buildings, embarked in their boats, and went down the river.

Having thus, after three years of labour and sorrow, attained his favourite wish—the reduction of Fort Duquesne and a total dispersion of the savages, Washington returned with joy to Williamsburgh, to take his seat in the legislature, to which he had been regularly chosen in his absence.

It is worthy of remark, because it happens but to few, that though he often failed of success, he never once lost the confidence of his country. Early aware of the importance of character, to those who wish to be useful, he omitted no honest act, thought no pains, no sacrifice of ease too great, to procure and preserve it. In the whole of that stupidly-managed war, as also another subsequent war, which was not much better conducted, he always took care to keep the public well informed as to the part which he had acted, or wished to act, in the affair. Not content, to know himself that he had acted wisely or bravely, he took care that the public should also know it; in order that if at any time an uproar should be made, the error might be charged to the real offender. If the legislature, or governor Dinwiddie, or general Braddock, or any other superior, with whom he had public concern, and character at stake, made propositions which he disliked, he would modestly point out their errors, predict their mischiefs, and thus wash his hands of all blame :—which documents, through the channel of numerous letters to his friends, were always laid before the people. Hence, for the ruinous consequences of the weakness and obstinacy of Dinwiddie and Braddock, not a breath of censure was ever blown on him. On the contrary, in the public mind, he always rose as high, or higher, than the others sunk. It was universally believed, that had he governed, in place of Dinwiddie, the fatal Indian war would not have lasted a campaign; and that on the hills of Monongahela, had Washington commanded in place of Braddock, the French and Indians would have been handled very differently. Such were the sentiments with which the public were prepared to receive him, on his return into their welcoming bosom. Wherever he went, homage always waited upon him, though always uncourted. The grey-headed rose up to do him honour, when he came into their company; and the young men, with sighs, often wished for a fame like his. Happy was the fairest lady of the land, who, at the crowded ball, could get colonel Washington for her partner. And even at the house where prayer is wont to be made, the eyes of beauty would sometimes wander from the cold reading preacher, to catch a livelier devotion from his "mind-illumined face,"—a face at once so dignified with virtue, and so sweetened with grace, that none could look on it without emotions very friendly to the heart; and sighs of sentiment, too delicate for description, were often seen to heave the snowy bosoms of the noblest dames.

At the head of all these stood the accomplished Mrs. Martha Custis, the beautiful and wealthy widow of Mr. John Custis. Her wealth was equal, at least, to one hundred thousand dollars! But her beauty was a sum far larger still. It was not the shallow boast of a fine skin, which time so quickly tarnishes, nor of those short-lived roses, which sometimes wither almost as soon as blown. But it sprung from the heart—from the divine and benevolent affections, which spontaneously gave to her eyes, her looks, her voice and her manners, such angelic charms, that I could never look on her, without exclaiming with the poet, O!

> "She was nearest heaven of all on earth I knew;
> And all but adoration was her due."

For two such kindred souls to love, it was only necessary that they should meet. Their friendship commenced with the first hour of their acquaintance, and was soon matured to marriage, which took place about the 27th year of Washington's life. His lady was, I believe, six months younger.

But that it is contrary to the rules of biography, to begin with the husband and end with the wife, I could relate of that most excellent lady those things which the public would greatly delight to hear. However, gratitude to that bright saint, now in heaven, who was my noblest benefactress, while I preached in her parish, compels me to say, that her virtues and charities were of that extensive and sublime sort, as fully to entitle her *hic jacet* to the following noble epitaph, a little altered, from one of the British poets.

> Underneath this marble hearse,
> Lies the subject of all verse.
> Custis' widow—great George's wife—
> Death! ere thou robb'st another life,
> Virtuous, fair, and good as she,
> Christ shall launch a dart at thee.

CHAPTER VIII.

Washington's mother has a very curious dream—it points to great coming trouble—a cloud arising in England—the causes of the revolutionary war.

WHEN a man begins to make a noise in the world, his relatives, (the Father, sometimes, but, always that tenderer parent, the Mother) are sure to recollect certain mighty odd dreams, which they had of him when he was a child. What rare dreams, for example, had the mothers of " Macedonia's madman, and the Swede," while pregnant with those butchers of the human race! Mrs. Washington also had her dream, which an excellent old Lady of Fredericks-burg assured me she had often heard her relate with great satisfaction; and, for the last time, but a few weeks before her death.

"I dreamt," said the Mother of Washington, " that I was sitting in the piazza of a large new house, into which we had but lately moved. George, at that time about five years old, was in the garden with his corn-stalk plough, busily running little furrows in the sand, in imitation of Negro Dick, a fine black boy, with whose ploughing George was so delighted that it was sometimes difficult to get him to his dinner. And so as I was sitting in the piazza at my work, I suddenly heard in my dream a kind of roaring noise on the eastern side of the house. On running out to see what was the matter, I beheld a dreadful sheet of fire bursting from the roof. The sight struck me with a horror which took away my strength, and threw me, almost senseless, to the ground. My husband and the servants, as I saw in my dream, soon came up; but, like myself, were so terrified at the sight, that they could make no attempt to extinguish the flames. In this most distressing state, the image of my little son came, I thought, to my mind more dear and tender than ever: and turning towards the garden where he was engaged with his little corn-stalk plough, I screamed out twice with all my might, George! George!—In a moment, as I thought, he threw down his mimic plough, and ran to me saying, "High! Ma! what makes you call so angry! 'an't I a good boy—don't I always run to you soon as I hear you call?" I could make no reply, but just threw up my arms towards the flame. He looked up and saw the house all on fire: but instead of bursting out a crying, as might have been expected from a child, he instantly brightened up, and seemed ready to fly to extinguish it. But first looking at me with great tenderness, he said, "Oh, Ma! don't be afraid: God Almighty will help us, and we shall soon put it out." His looks and words revived our spirits in so wonderful a manner, that we all instantly set about to assist him. A ladder was presently brought, on which, as I saw in my dream, he ran up with the nimbleness of a squirrel; and the servants supplied him with water, which he threw on the fire from an American gourd. But that growing weaker, the flame appeared to gain ground, breaking forth and roaring most dreadfully, which so frightened the servants, that many of them, like persons in despair, began to leave him. But he, still undaunted, continued to ply it with water, animating the servants at the same time, both by his word and actions. For a long time the contest appeared very doubtful: but at length a venerable old man, with a tall cap and an iron rod in his hand, like a lightning rod, reached out to him a curious little trough, like a wooden shoe! On receiving this, he redoubled his exertions, and soon extinguished the fire. Our joy on the occasion was unbounded. But he, on the contrary, showing no more of transport now than of terror before, looked rather sad at sight of the great harm that had been done. Then I saw in my dream that after some time spent as in deep thought, he called out with much joy, " Well, Ma! now if you and the family will but consent, we can make a far better roof than this ever was; a roof of such a quality, that if well kept together, it will last for ever; but if you take it apart, you will make the house ten thousand times worse than it was before."

This, though certainly a very curious dream, needs no Daniel to interpret it; especially if we take Mrs. Washington's new house, for the young Colony Government—the fire on its east side, for North's civil war—the gourd which Washington first employed, for the American three and six months enlistments—the old man with his cap and iron rod, for Doctor Franklin—the shoe-like vessel which he reached to Washington, for the Sabot or wooden-shoed nation, the French, whom Franklin courted a long time for America—and the new roof proposed by Washington, for a staunch honest Republic—that " equal government," which, by guarding alike the welfare of all, ought by all to be so heartily beloved as to endure for ever.

Had it been appointed unto any man to quaff unmingled happiness in this life, George Washington had been that man. For where is that pleasurable ingredient with which his cup was not full and overflowing?

Crowned with honours—laden with riches—blest with health—and in the joyous prime of 27, sharing each rural sweet in the society of a charming woman who doated on him, he surely bid fair to spend his days and nights of life in ceaseless pleasure.—But ah!—as sings the sweet bard of Zion,

> Our days, alas! our mortal days,
>   Are short and wretched too!
> "Evil and few!" the Patriarch says,
>   And well the Patriarch knew!
> 'Tis but at best, a narrow bound,
>   That Heaven allots to men;
> And pains and sins run through the round
>   Of three-score years and ten!

From this, the universal lot, not Washington himself could obtain exemption. For in the midst of his favourite labours, of the plough and pruning-hook, covering his extensive farms with all the varied delights of delicious fruits and golden grain, of lowing herds and snowy flocks, he was suddenly called on by his country, to turn his plough-share into a sword, and go forth to meet a torrent of evils which threatened her. The fountain of those evils, whence at length flowed the great civil war, which for ever separated Britain and her children, I proceed now briefly to state.

After the reduction of Canada, the British officers who commanded on that expedition, came to Boston and New York, on a visit to their American brethren in arms, who had served with them in that war. Soon as their arrival was announced, the Americans flew to meet and welcome them. They were paraded through the streets as the saviours of the land—the doors of all were thrown open to receive them—and every day, during their stay, was spent in feasting and public dinners, which, for the sake of their beloved guests, were made as splendid as possible, though always through the aid of obliging neighbours. The rooms glittered with borrowed plate—wines of every vintage sparkled on the crowded side-boards —while the long extended tables were covered with the finest fish and flesh, succeeded by the richest desserts. The British officers were equally charmed and astonished at such elegant hospitality, and, on their return to England, gave full scope to their feelings. They painted the colonial wealth in the colourings of romance ; and spoke of the Americans as a people, who, in comparison of the British, lived like kings.

Thus, American hospitality, by a strange perversion, had nearly destroyed American Liberty ! For, from that time, the British ministry began to look upon the Americans with an evil eye, and to devise ways and means to make us "bear a part of their burdens!" But what did they mean by this? Did they mean to acknowledge us as sons of Britons; equally free and independent with our brethren in England? and, like them, allowed a representation in Parliament, who should freely vote our money for the common cause?

Oh no! an idea so truly British and honourable, was not at all in their thoughts. We were not to be treated as brothers, but as slaves! over whom an unconditional right was claimed, to tax and take our property at pleasure!!!

Reader, if you be a Briton, be a Briton still—preserve the characteristic calm and candour of a Briton. I am not about to say one word against your nation. No! I know them too well: and thank God, I can say, after several years residence among them, I believe them to be as honest, charitable, and magnanimous a people as any under the canopy of Heaven. I am about to speak of the Ministry only, who certainly, at that time, were a most ambitious and intriguing junto, who by bad means had attained power; and by worse were endeavouring to extend it, even to the destruction of both American and British Liberty, as the excellent Mr. Pitt charged them.—No Englishman can desire fuller evidence than this one tyrannical claim made against us by Lord North— "taxation without representation!!" As a plea for such despotic doing, North and his creatures began with boldly trumpeting the wonderful kindness they had conferred on America. "They, it seems, "first discovered the country!—they settled it—they always had defended it. It was their blood—their treasure —their ships and sailors, and soldiers, that created the British colonies!!

O dear!—and what then!—why, to be sure, after having done such mighty things for the Americans, they had as clear a right to their gold and silver, as a butcher has to the hair and hides of his cattle!

This language was actually carried into Parliament! where a Mr. Charles Townsend, to enforce the stamp. act, cried out, " Who are these Americans? Are they not our children, planted by our care, nourished by our indulgence, and protected by our arms?

At this the brave Colonel Barre, with cheeks inflamed with virtuous indignation, thus thundered forth against the insolent speechifier. " They planted by your care! No, sir: your oppressions planted them in America. They fled from your tyranny to a then uncultivated and inhospitable country, where they exposed themselves to all the evils which a wilderness, filled with blood-thirsty savages, could threaten. And yet, actuated by true English love of liberty, they thought all these evils light in comparison with what they had suffered in their own country, and from you, who ought to have been their friends.

" They nourished by your indulgence! No, sir! they grew by your neglect. As soon as you began to indulge them, that boasted indulgence was to send them hungry packs of your own creatures, to spy out their liberties!—to misrepresent their actions—and to prey upon their substance!—Yes, sir, you sent them men, whose behaviour has often caused the blood of those sons of Liberty to recoil within them— men promoted by you to the highest seats of justice, in that country, who, to my knowledge, had good cause to dread a court of justice in their own!—They protected by your arms!—No, sir! They have nobly taken up arms in your defence ; have exerted a most heroic valour, amidst their daily labours, for the defence of a country whose frontier was drenched in blood, while its interior parts gave up all their savings for our emolument !"

All this was very true. For the Americans had not only planted, but in a great measure protected themselves. In the French and Indian war, from '55 to '63, they lost nearly 30,000 of their stoutest young men! And by regular returns it appears that Massachusetts alone expended about 50,000*l.* sterling in that time !!! And moreover, they had never hesitated for a moment to furnish to the last man and the last shilling whatever Britain had required.

But, alas! what signifies right against might! When a king wants money for his own pride, or for his hungry relations, and when his ministers want stakes for their gaming tables, or diamond necklaces for their mistresses, they will have it, though plundered colonies should lack bread and spelling books for their children. For in the year '63, when the lamp of God was burning with peculiar brightness in our land, and both Britain and her colonies enjoyed a measure of blessings seldom indulged to the most favoured nations—when, at the very mention of Old England, our hearts leaped for joy, as at the name of a great and venerable mother, and that mother felt equal transport at thoughts of us, her flourishing colonies—when all the produce of these vast and fertile regions was poured into her beloved lap, and she in return, not allowing us the trouble to make even a hob-nail, heaped our families with all the necessaries and elegancies of her ingenious artists— when, though far separated by an ocean's roar, we were yet so united by love and mutual helpfulness, that the souls of Columbus, Raleigh, and Smith, looking down from Heaven, with joy beheld the consummation of all their labours and wishes! At that happy period, lord North brought in a bill to tax the colonies, without allowing us a voice in their councils!! The colonies were thunderstruck: and Britain herself groaning through all her islands, " gave signs of woe, that all was lost !"

Doctor Franklin, who was then in England as a colony agent, on hearing that this most iniquitous bill had actually passed both houses, and was ratified by the king, wrote to a friend in America in these words—" The sun of our liberty is set. You must all now light up the double candles of Industry and

Economy. But, above all things, encourage the young people to marry and raise up children as fast as they can."

Meaning, that America, yet too weak to resist the chains which a wicked ministry were forging for her, should instantly fly to heaven-ordered marriage, for her heroic youth, to rend the ignominious bonds from their own and their father's arms.

But the sons of Columbia, though few in number, had too long enjoyed the sweets of Liberty and property to part with them so tamely, because a king and his minions had ordered it. No! blessed be God, their conduct was such as to strike the world with this glorious truth, that a brave people, who know their rights, are not to be enslaved.

For, soon as it was told in America, that the stamp-act had passed, the people rose up against it as one man—the old grudges between churchmen and dissenters were instantly forgotten—every man looked to his fellow as to a brother for aid against the coming slavery—their looks on each other were as lightnings in a parched forest—the sacred fire kindled, and ran from end to end of the continent. In every colony the people rushed into patriotic societies.... reminded each other of their rights.... denounced the stamp-act as a most audacious infringement—burnt in effigy the promoters of it—destroyed the houses of those degenerated Americans who had received the stamps to sell—and menaced loudly a non-intercourse with Britian, if the act was not immediately repealed!

This spirited behaviour filled all England with amazement. Every man there, no matter what his principles or politics, felt it to the very quick. The manufacturers and merchants trembled; the tories raved; the whigs rejoiced, and, with the great Pitt and Burke at their head, publicly applauded the Americans, and denounced the stamp-act as entirely contrary to the spirit of British freedom. In short,

the cry against it was so loud, both in England and
America, that the ministry, covered with shame,
were obliged to give way, and abandon the project.

The cloud, which had hung so dark over the two
countries, being thus happily scattered, many began
to cherish the hope, that we should have a clear sky
again, and that the former golden days would soon
return. But alas! those golden days were gone, to
return no more! Government had shown the
cloven foot—and America had taken a fright which
nothing but whole years of kindliest treatment could
ever sooth. But, unfortunately, the ministry were
in no humour to show that kindness. Long accustomed to speak of the Americans as a pack of
"convicts, whom by transportation, they had kindly
saved from the gallows," instead of giving them
credit for their late spirited behaviour, they considered it as the height of audacity: and though from
necessity they had yielded to their demands, they
were determined to have revenge on the first
opportunity. That opportunity was too soon afforded.

It should have been stated, that with the duty on
stamp paper, similar duties had been laid on glass,
tea, &c. &c., all of which had been repealed with the
stamp act, except that on tea. This the ministry
had artfully retained: partly to cover the shame of
their defeat, but chiefly in hopes of familiarizing the
Americans with taxation. For though Lord North
was never, that I know of, charged with being a
wizard, yet did he not lack sense to know that if he
could but prevail on the young Mammoth to submit
to a tax, though as small as a Gnat, he soon should
bring him to swallow a Camel! But glory to God!
the Americans had too much of British blood, to
allow an unconstitutional tax in any shape or size.
Independent and coy as the birds of their forests,
they would not suffer a stranger's hand even to
touch the sacred nest of their rights. As soon there-

fore, as the ministry began, in 1773, to order "the collection of taxes on tea," the colonies took fire again: and the old flame of '53 was completely rekindled throughout the continent. But still in the very storm and tempest of their rage, they never lost sight of the respect due their mother country. Their numerous letters and petitions to the King, to the Parliament, and to the people of Britain, all, all, breathe the full spirit of dutiful children, and of loving brothers. In terms the most modest and pathetic, they state the extreme injustice and barbarity of such measures—their total inconsistency with the spirit of the British Constitution—their positive inadmissibility into America—or, in that event, the certainty of a civil war, with all its fatal effects on the two countries.

Tempered with meekness, and pointed with truth, their arguments reach the hearts of the British patriots, who all fly in eager myriads to extinguish the kindling flames of civil war. Foremost of this noble band is seen the venerable form of Chatham. Though worn with years and infirmities, he quits his bed; and, muffled up in flannels and furs, crawls to the house of lords, to give his last advice, and yet avert, if possible, the impending ruin. He rises to speak. A solemn silence prevails, while the looks of the crowded audience are bending forward upon him, to catch the accents of his magic tongue. His eyes are upon the ground: but his thoughts are not there: they are travelling like sun-beams over all the earth. Britain and America, with all their population and interests, lie open before his vast mind, with the varied evils of the threatened war. In Britain he beholds a fearful pause in the pulse of industry and joy—the loom is still—the anvil re sounds no more—while the harbours, late alive with bustling business and cheerful songs, now crowded with silent dismantled ships, present a scene of national mourning. In the colonies he sees the plains, lately crowned with joyful harvests, now covered with armed bands of Britons and Americans rushing to murderous battle—while in Europe, the proud Spaniard, the sarcastic Gaul, and broad grinning Hollander, with shrugs and sneers enjoy the coming fray, as a welcome prelude to the downfall of their hated rival. He next paints the Americans as native sons of Britain—and, at once, enthusiastic lovers of liberty and of their mother country—ready, as her children, to give her every thing; but, as her slaves, nothing. Though harshly treated, they still love her, and wish for nothing so much as a hearty reconciliation, and a glad return of all the former friendships and blessings. At thought of this most desirable of all events, the parent soul of the great orator is stirred within him, his angel frame trembles with strong feeling, which heaves his labouring bosom, and swells his changeful face. At length his powerful words break forth.

"For God's sake then, my lords, let the way be instantly opened for reconciliation. I say instantly; or it will be too late for ever. The Americans tell you—and remember, it is the language of the whole continent—they tell you, they will never submit to be taxed without their own consent. They insist on a repeal of your laws. They do not ask it as a favour. They claim it as a right. They demand it. —And I tell you the acts must be repealed. They will be repealed. You cannot enforce them. But bare repeal will not satisfy this enlightened and spirited people. What! satisfy them by repealing a bit of paper—by repealing a piece of parchment! No! you must declare you have no right to tax them. Then they may trust you—then they will come into you. There are, my lords, three millions of whigs in America. Three millions of whigs, with arms in their hands, are a formidable body! There are, I trust, double that number of whigs in England. And I hope the whigs in both countries will join and make a common cause. They are united by the strongest ties of sentiment and interest; and will therefore, I hope, fly to support their brethren. In this most alarming and distracted state of our affairs, though borne down by a cruel disease, I have crawled to this house, my lords, to give you my best advice, which is, to beseech his majesty that orders may instantly be dispatched to General Gage to remove the troops from Boston. Their presence is a source of perpetual irritation and suspicion to those people. How can they trust you, with the bayonet at their breasts? They have all the reason in the world to believe that you mean their death or slavery. Let us then set to this business in earnest. There is no time to be lost. Every moment is big with danger. Nay, while I am now speaking, the decisive blow may be struck, and millions involved in the dreadful consequences! The very first drop of blood that is drawn, will make a wound perhaps never to be healed—a wound of such rancorous malignity, as will, in all probability, mortify the whole body, and hasten, both on England and America, that dissolution to which all nations are destined."

Here was a speech, sufficient, one would have thought, to stop the career of the maddest politicians. —But neither this, nor the advice of lord Camden, nor the numerous and pathetic addresses from London, Liverpool, and Jamaica, could produce the least change in the views of the ministry. " Let the Americans," said lord Gower with a sneer, " sit talking about their natural rights! their divine rights! and such stuff! we will send them over a few regiments of grenadiers to help their consultations!" Thus high-toned was the language of ministry, and thus stoutly bent on the submission of the Americans. Indeed, in some instances, they would not honour them so far as to give their " humble petitions" a reading; but consigned them to what the whig opposition pleasantly called, " the committee of oblivion."

The tea-tax was, of course, at any rate to be collected. But as there could be no tax without tea, nor tea unless it was sent, several ships of that obnoxious weed were purposely dispatched for America. Lord Fairfax happened to be at Mount Vernon when Washington received advice from a friend in London that the tea-ships were about to sail. . . . " Well, my lord," said he, " and so the ships, with the gun-powder tea, are, it seems, on their way to America !"

" Well, but colonel, why do you call it gunpowder tea."

" Why, I am afraid, my lord," replied Washington, " it will prove inflammable, and produce an explosion that will shake both countries."

The event corresponded with Washington's prediction. Looked on as sent to insult and enslave them, the ships were every where received with the heartiest curses of the people, who quickly boarded them—in some places furiously emptying their fragrant cargoes into the flashing deep ;—in others, sternly ordering the captains to depart, under the penalty of being instantly tucked up to the yard arms.

On the arrival of this news in England, the countenance of the minister was dark with fury ; and he proceeded, without delay, to mix up for the colonies a cup of fiery indignation, of which Boston, it seems, was to have the largest dose. As that most undutiful child had always led off the dance in outrage and rebellion against the parent state, it was determined that she should pay the piper for old and new . . . that her purse should answer for all the tea that had been destroyed . . . that her luxuriant trade, which had made her so wanton, should be taken from her—and, that, in spite of her high looks and proud stomach, she should sit on the stool of repentance, until his gracious majesty, George III. should be pleased to pronounce her pardon ! !

On the receipt of this intelligence at Boston, the passions of the people flew up, five hundred degrees above blood-heat! throughout the continent the fever raged with equal fury. The colonies all extolled Boston for the firmness with which she had asserted her chartered rights.... Liberal contributions were made for her relief: and this ministerial attack on her liberties, was considered as an attack on the liberties of the whole, which were now thought to be in such danger, as loudly to call for a general congress from all the colonies, to deliberate on their common interest. This most unkingly body commenced its session in Philadelphia, September 5th, 1774. They began with publishing a bill of rights, wherein they repeated " their loyalty and love to the mother country, together with an earnest wish for constitutional dependence on her. But, at the same time, they begged leave to assure her, that though she, in her excessive fondness, might suffer herself to be bound and insulted by North and Bute, and other Philistine lords, yet they, for their parts, were resolved, like true sons of British Sampsons, to rise and fight to the last locks of their heads. They asserted, and begged leave to do it pretty roundly too, as it was now high time to speak plain, that by the immutable laws of nature — by the principles of the British constitution — and by their several charters, they had a right to liberty, the liberty of British subjects —that their ever honored fathers, at the time of their emigration to this country, were entitled to all the rights of freemen—and since, by such emigration they had neither forfeited nor surrendered these rights—that they their children, were determined, at the risk of every thing short of their eternal salvation, to defend and to transmit them entire to their innocent and beloved offspring."

Millions of choice spirits in England, Scotland, and Ireland, cried out " that's well said! and may God's arms strike with our American brethren!"

This was coming to the point, and produced the effect that might have been expected. For, instantly all exportation of arms and ammunition to America was prohibited—large reinforcements were sent to the king's troops at Boston—and every step was taken to compel the colonies to submission. This filled up the measure of American hatred to the ministry, and called forth the most vigorous preparations for war. Every ounce of gunpowder was husbanded like so much gold-dust. Powder-mills and musket-manufactories were erected in most of the colonies; while others, not liking this slow way of doing things, laid violent hands at once upon all the king's arms and ammunition that could be found.

The tremendous cloud of civil war was now ready to burst: and April the 19th, 1775, was the fatal day marked out by mysterious heaven, for tearing away the stout infant colonies from the long-loved paps of the old mother country. Early that morning, general Gage, whose force in Boston was augmented to 10,000 men, sent a detachment of 1000 to destroy some military stores which the Americans had collected in the town of Concord, near Lexington. On coming to the place, they found the town militia assembled on the green near the road. "Throw down your arms, and disperse, you rebels," was the cry of Pitcairn the British officer; which was immediately followed by a general discharge of the soldiers; whereby eight of the Americans were killed, and several wounded. The provincials retired. But finding that the British still continued their fire, they returned it with good interest; and soon strewed the green with the dead and wounded. Such fierce discharges of musketry produced the effect that might have been expected in a land of freemen, who saw their gallant brothers suddenly engaged in the strife of death. Never before had the bosoms of the swains experienced such a tumult of heroic passions. Then hrowing aside the implements of husbandry, and

BATTLE OF LEXINGTON.

leaving their teams in the half-finished furrows, they flew to their houses; snatched up their arms; and bursting from their wild shrieking wives and children, hasted to the glorious field, where LIBERTY, heaven-born goddess, was to be bought for blood. Pouring in now from every quarter, were seen crowds of sturdy peasants, with flushed cheeks and flaming eyes, eager for battle! Even age itself forgot its wonted infirmities: and hands, long palsied with years, threw aside the cushioned crutch, and grasped the deadly firelock. Fast as they came up, their ready muskets began to pour the long red streams of fiery vengeance. The enemy fell back, apalled! The shouting farmers, swift closing on their rear, followed their steps with death, while the British, as fast as they could load, wheeling on their pursuers, returned the deadly platoons. Like some tremendous whirlwind, whose roaring sweep all at once darkens the day, riding the air in tempests; so sudden and terrible, amidst clouds of dust, and smoke, and flame, the flight of Britain's warriors thundered along the road. But their flight was not in safety. Every step of their retreat was stained with the trickling crimson. Every hedge or fence by which they pas-sed, took large toll of hostile carcasses. They would, in all probability, have been cut off to a man, had not general Gage, luckily recollected, that, born of Britons, these Yankees might possess some of the family valour; and therefore sent 1000 men to sup-port the detachment. This reinforcement met the poor fellows, faint with fear and fatigue, and brought them safely off to Boston.

In this their first field, the American farmers gleaned of the British about sixty-three, in slain, and two hundred and eighty wounded and prisoners. The fire of civil discord now broke out a roaring flame: and, with equal ardour, both parties hastened to clap on the "kettle of war."

National prejudices ought to be scouted from the

7*

face of the earth. Colonel Grant actually said in parliament, that " with five regiments he could march through all America!!!" Oh! had that profound philosopher but beheld the scrub race above, he might have learned two things—first, that he was never born to be a prophet. And secondly, that as it is not to this or that country exclusively, that we are to look for brave men, but in every country where the people are accustomed to breathe the proud air of liberty, and to rejoice in the sweet fruits of their labours as all their own.

Soon as the battle of Lexington was told to the astonished ministry in England, a grand caucus of lords was held, to consider the best ways and means to bring the rebels to their senses. " One spoke after this manner, and another after that. Presently up rose lord George Germaine, and with all Moloch in his looks, hurled the curses of Amalek against the Americans. " Vengeance! gentlemen!" he cried, " vengeance! your insulted island—your wounded honour—your murdered countrymen—all cry havoc! and bid slip the dogs of war. Gods! can we sit debating here, when rank rebellion lords it over our colonies, and the tongues of rebel curs are red in the blood of our bravest soldiers slain. No! let our swift-avenging armies fly across the ocean, and lighting like a tornado on the rebel continent, from end to end, with fire and sword sweep both town and country before them."

Here the celebrated Mr. Wilkes, in the spirit of a true Briton, roared out: " Aye, that's right! that's right! lord George! that's exactly according to our old English proverb——the greater the coward, the crueller the devil!"

" Coward! Sir!" replied lord George, black with rage. " Coward! what do you mean by that, sir?"

" I mean, sir," returned Mr. Wilkes, " that the hero who could not stand fire on the plains of Minden, does well to advise fire and sword in the woods of America."

Upon this, the unlovely names of liar and scoundrel were exchanged with a freedom which showed that in the quarrel with America the passions of the two parties knew no bounds. Happily for America, this spirit of Mr. Wilkes was not peculiar to himself. Thousands of enlightened and virtuous whigs breathed it with equal ardour. The gallant duke of Buckingham, on hearing how bravely the Americans had behaved at Lexington, exclaimed, "Well, thank God! there are yet some veins in the world that beat high with British blood!"

Lord Effingham, also, being required to take up arms against the Americans, returned his sword to the king, saying, "he had received it on oath, to maintain the cause of justice, not of oppression!!"

But though the right heads in England were numerous, they were not sufficiently so to direct the wrong heads. A feeble minister, and his puny lordlings, still held the reins: and though, compared with the great nation which they governed, they seemed but as monkeys on the back of a mammoth, yet they had, too long, the fatal art so to blindfold and goad the noble animal, as to make her run riot over her own children, and crush thousands of them into their bloody graves.

On this day, June 12, 1775, General Gage issued his proclamation of rebellion, with threats of heaviest vengeance against the rebels; extending however in the king's name, the golden sceptre of mercy to all true penitents, Samuel Adams, and John Hancock, excepted. These gentlemen, by their extraordinary zeal in the cause of liberty, had so mortally offended the ministry, that nothing short of their lives could make atonement. Orders were sent privately to General Gage, to seize and hang them in Boston, or to send them over in irons to be hung in England. But God gave his angels charge of them, so that not a hair of their heads was hurt.

The British, 10,000 strong, were still in Boston,

where, ever since the affair of Concord, they had been surrounded by an army of 20,000 provincials, all so eager to take the city by storm, that it was with the greatest difficulty their officers could restrain them.

How adorable the goodness of God for ordering that the ministerial attack on our liberties, should fall on the populous and high-toned New-Englanders! The heroic spirit with which they repelled it, should to eternity, endear them to their southern brethren.

CHAPTER IX.

Battle of Bunker's-hill—of Sullivan's Island—Declaration of Independence—Defeat of the Americans on Long-Island—Howe threatens violently—Times squally.

——And fame of Bunker's hill endure,
Till time itself shall be no more.

This hill of fame still lifts its yellow brow, half hid in sedge, on the plains of Charlestown—a lovely port north of Boston, to which it is united by an elegant bridge. To confine the British as closely as possible to Boston, the American generals, on the night of June 16, despatched 1500 men to throw up an entrenchment on Bunker's-hill. The party did not begin their work till about 12 o'clock; but exerted such a spirit, that, by day-break, they had surrounded themselves with a tolerably decent ditch—without embrasures indeed, because they had no cannon to stare through them; nor even a bayonet to bristle over its ridges.

Soon as the rosy morn appeared, they were discovered by the British men of war, which quickly saluted them with their great guns and mortars. But, regardless of shells and shot, the dauntless Yankees still drank their Switchel* and plied their work.

Finding that his ships of war, with all their thunders, had not been able to dislodge them, Gage ordered to their aid 3000 men with a train of artillery, under command of Generals Howe and Pigot. By twelve o'clock they were all safely landed on the Charlestown side, near Bunker's-hill, the destined place of storm. An interesting scene is now about to open—for not only the British and American armies from the neighbouring heights, are eagerly looking on; but all the surrounding country, timely alarmed, are running together, in terror, to behold the coming fight. Among the crowding spectators are seen thousands of tender females, with panting bosoms and watery eyes, fixed upon the fields below, anxiously waiting the fate of their brothers, fathers, and husbands. After a hurried moment spent in forming, the British troops began to advance in heavy columns, with all the martial pomp of flying colours and rattling drums. At the same time, by order of Gage, the beautiful port of Charlestown, of 300 fine buildings, with a tall steepled church, was wrapped in flames, roaring like distant thunder, and tossed on eddying winds in fiery billows to the clouds—while, far and wide, the adjoining plains are covered with British soldiers in crimson regimentals and shining arms, moving on the attack with incessant discharges of muskets and great guns. Close, on the brow of the hill, appears the little fort, dimly seen through smoke, and waved over by one solitary flag, and very unlike to stand the shock of so powerful an armament. But the Americans are all wound up to the height of the enthusiasm of Liberty: and,

---

* A mild and moralising malmsey, made of molasses and water, which the prudent Yankees drink, to the great benefit of their health and senses, while too many of their southern neighbours are be-fooling and be-poisoning themselves with grog.

lying close behind their works, with fowling pieces loaded with ball and buckshot, wait impatiently for the approaching enemy. Their brave countrymen, Putnam and Warren, are in the fort, constantly reminding them of that glorious inheritance, Liberty, which they received from their gallant fathers, and now owe to their own dear children. "Don't throw away a single shot, my brave fellows," said old Putnam. "Don't throw away a single shot; but take good aim: nor touch a trigger, till you can see the whites of their eyes."

This steady reserve of fire, even after the British had come up within pistol-shot, led them to hope that the Americans did not mean to resist, and many of their friends on the heights had nearly given up all for lost. But as soon as the enemy were advanced within the fatal distance marked, all at once a thousand triggers were drawn: and a sheet of fire, wide as the whole front of the breast-work, bursted upon them with most ruinous effect. The British instantly came to a halt—still keeping up their fire—but altogether at random and ineffectual, like men in a panic. While full exposed, within point-blank shot, ranks on ranks fell before the American marksmen, as the heavy-eared corn before the devouring hail storm, when with whirlwind rage it smites the trembling earth, and rushes on, smoking and roaring through the desolated fields. The enemy still maintained their ground like Britons, though all in front was nothing but one wide destructive flash; and nought around but heaps of their shrieking, dying comrades. But in a few minutes the slaughter became so general, that they could stand it no longer, but broke and fled in the utmost disorder, to the shore side; and some even took refuge in their boats! Their officers with some difficulty brought them back to a second charge, when the Americans, waiting till they had come up within a few rods of the fort, recommenced their fire, with a mortality which broke and drove

BATTLE OF BUNKER'S HILL.

them again. Some of the officers attempted to bring them on a third time, but others cried out, "that it was no better than murder!" It is probable they would hardly have made another effort, had not the generals Clinton and Burgoyne, spectators of their defeat, hastened over from Boston with fresh troops to their aid.

The Americans, being nearly destitute of ammunition, and attacked by such superior force, were obliged to retreat, which they did in tolerable order, but not till they had given the enemy, as they mounted the works, their last cartridges, and to some of them the buts of their guns—for want of bayonets. The British, 'tis true, by such great advantage of numbers and weapons, gained the day; but sung no te deum. To have given 1350 men killed and wounded, for a poor ditch of 12 hours labour, seemed to them a bargain hardly worth thanking God for.

Among the Heroes whom this day immolated on the altar of Patriotism, was Dr. Joseph Warren, whose memory will be held sacred as long as gratitude or honour live among men. The British lost Major Pitcairn, author of the murders at Lexington, a few weeks before!

During the autumn and winter of 1775, Washington could effect nothing against the British, but to hold them close confined in Boston, where the scurvy prevailed, and proved very fatal. To remedy this evil, immense quantities of live stock and vegetables were shipped from Britain—5,000 fat oxen; 14,000 sheep—12,000 hogs, with 22,000 pounds sterling worth of sour-crout!!! And nearly the same amount in hay, oats and beans, for a single regiment of cavalry!! "Blessed are the meek!" for they shall save a world of expense.

In consequence of some disturbances this year, in South Carolina, in favour of the ministry, Sir Peter Parker was dispatched with nine ships of war, and a large land force, commanded by Clinton and Cornwallis, to make an attempt on Charleston, the capital. Before the ships could be brought to pay their respects to the town, they must, it seems, pass a little fort on Sullivan's Island. This, however, being defended only by raw militia, was hardly looked on as an obstacle. Happily for America, the command of the fort had been committed to General Moultrie; for the chief in command, Gen. Charles Lee, though otherwise brave, was ever in the frights at the thought of a British man of war; and for a general, much too free in lending his fear to others. For, while Moultrie was showing him the fort, and in the language of a fiery patriot was boasting what handsome resistance he hoped it would make; Lee with infinite scorn replied, "Pshaw! a mere slaughter house! a mere slaughter house! a British man of war will knock it about your ears in half an hour!" He even proposed to abandon the fort! The courage of one man saved Charleston, and perhaps the State. That fortunate man was John Rutledge, Esq., governor of South Carolina. He insisted that the fort should be defended to the last extremity. Moultrie was called in. "Well, General Moultrie," said Gov. Rutledge, "what do you think of giving up the fort!" Moultrie could scarcely suppress his indignation. "No man, sir," said he to Lee, "can have a higher opinion of the British ships and seamen than I have. But there are others who love the smell of gunpowder as well as they do; and give us but plenty of powder and ball, sir, and let them come on as soon as they please." His courage was quickly put to the test; for about 10 o'clock, on the 28th of June, in the glorious 1776, Sir Peter Parker, with seven tall ships formed his line, and bearing down within point-blank shot of the fort, let go his anchors and began a tremendous fire. At every thundering blast he fondly hoped to see the militia take to the sands like frightened rats from an

old barn on fire. But, widely different from his
hopes, the militia stood their ground, firm as the
Black-jacks of their land; and levelling their four-
and-twenty pounders with good aim, bored the old
hearts of oak through and through at every fire.
Their third broadside carried away the springs on
the cables of the commodore's ship, which immediately swung around right stern upon the guns of the
fort—" Hurra! my sons of thunder," was instantly
the cry along the American battery, "look handsomely to the commodore! now my boys, for your
best respects to the commodore!" Little did the
commodore thank them for such respects; for in a
short time he had 60 of his brave crew lying lifeless
on his decks, and his cockpit stowed with the wounded. At one period of the action, the quarter-deck
was cleared of every soul, except Sir Peter himself.
Nor was he entirely excused; for an honest cannon
ball, by way of broad hint that it was out of character for a Briton to fight against liberty, rudely
snatched away the bag of his silk breeches. Thus
Sir Peter had the honour to be the first, and I believe
the only Sans Culotte ever heard of in American
natural history!!

The Americans stood the fire like SALAMANDERS;
for the neighbouring shores were lined with thousands
of their dearest relatives, anxiously looking on! the
British tars, poor fellows! had no sisters, mothers,
nor wives, spectators of their strife; but fought, notwithstanding, with their wonted heroism. Long
accustomed to mastery in battles with the French,
and greatly out-numbering the fort both in men and
guns, they counted on certain victory; and though
dreadfully handled, scorned to yield. Immense
were the exertions on both sides; and while the
powder of the fort lasted, the conflict was awfully
grand—From ships to fort, and from fort to ships
again, all below seemed one stream of solid fire; all
above, one vast mountain of smoke darkening the

day, while unintermitted bursts of thunder deafened all ears, and far around shook both land and sea.

The heroes in the fort won immortal honour. One brave fellow, a Sergeant Jasper, observing the flag-staff shot away, jumped down from the fort on the beach, in the hottest fury of the battle, and snatching up he flag, returned it to its place, streaming defi-ance, with a—"Hurra, my boys, liberty and America for ever." Governor Rutledge rewarded him with a sword. Another Sergeant, M'Donald, while roaring away with his 24 pounder, was terribly shattered by a cannon ball. When about to expire, he lifted up his dying eyes and said—"My brave countrymen, I die; but don't let the cause of Liberty die with me." Now louder and louder still, peal on peal, the Ame-rican thunder burst forth with earth-trembling crash-es: and the British ships, after a long and gallant struggle, hauled off with a good fortnight's worth of work for surgeons, carpenters and riggers.

Sir Peter was so dumb-founded by this drubbing, that it took him full eight-and-forty-hours to recover his stomach for his beef and pudding. So wonderful-ly had it let him down, that even his black pilots grew impudent upon him. For as he was going out over the bar, he called to Cudjo (a black fellow, a pilot who was sounding the depth of the water)——"Cud-jo! (says he) what water have you got there?"

"What water, massa? what water? why salt water, be sure, sir?—sea water alway salt water, an't he, massa?"

"You black rascal, I knew it was salt water. I only wanted to know how much water you have there?"

"How much water here, massa? how much water here! God bless me, massa! where I going get quart pot for measure him?"

This was right down impudence; and Cudjo richly deserved a rope's end for it; but Sir Peter, a good natured man, was so tickled with the idea of measuring the Atlantic ocean with a quart pot, that he broke into a hearty laugh, and ordered Cudjo a stiff drink of grog.

'Twas the celebrated Samuel Chase, the Demosthenes of Maryland, who first taught the startled vaults of Congress hall to re-echo the name of Independence. After enumerating many a glaring instance of ministerial violation of American rights—on all of which George III., the expected father of his people, had looked with a most unfatherly calmness—his countenance became like the dark stormy cloud edged with lightning—then swinging his arm in the air, with a tremendous stamp and voice of thunder, that made the hollow dome resound, he swore——a mighty oath, "that he owed no allegiance to the king of England !"

Many in Congress trembled at hearing such a speech; and, on mention of Independence, felt the pang which nature feels when soul and body are parting. But fearing that "true friendship could never grow again, where wounds of deadly hate had pierced so deep," they at length resolved to part. The gentlemen appointed by Congress to frame the declaration of Independence, were THOMAS JEFFERSON, JOHN ADAMS, DR. FRANKLIN, R. SHERMAN and R. LIVINGSTON. On hearing their nomination to a task so high and arduous, they met; and after some conversation on the subject, parted, under the agreement that each of their number should draft his own declaration, and read it next day, in rotation to the rest. At the fixed hour next day, they met—but "who should read first," was the question. Mr. Jefferson was fixed on; and, after much importunity, consented to read his form, which had the honour to give such complete satisfaction, that none other was read.

A few days after this, Lord Howe came upon the coast with a forest of men of war and transports. shading far and wide the frightened ocean, and

8*

bearing nearly 40,000 men, British, Hessians, and Waldeckers. Supposing that this had intimidated the American commander, Lord Howe wrote a letter to him, directed—" George Washington, Esq." This the general refused to receive ! looking on it as an insult to Congress under whom he had the honour to bear the commission of Commander in Chief, and should have been addressed as such. General Howe then sent an officer (Colonel Patterson) to converse with him on the subject of reconciliation—Having heard what he had to say, Washington replied, " by what has yet appeared, sir, you have no power but to grant pardons. But we who have committed no faults, want no pardons ; for we are only fighting for our rights as the descendants of Englishmen."

The unfortunate defeat of Long-Island now took place on August 28th, which though the hottest day in the year, had like to have been the freezing point in the American affairs. For on this day, the British, with an infinite superiority of force, after having defeated the Americans with great loss, were investing the slender remains of their army ; and had actually broke ground within six hundred yards of the little redoubt that feebly covered their front. Soon as it was dark, Washington ordered the troops to convey their baggage and artillery to the water side, whence it was transported over a broad ferry all night long, with amazing silence and order. Providentially a thick fog continued next morning till ten o'clock ; when that passed away, and the sun broke out, the British were equally surprised and enraged to see the rear guard with the last of the baggage in their boats, and out of all danger.

Lord Howe, supposing that such a run of misfortunes must have put congress into a good humour to think about peace, signified a willingness to have a grand talk on the subject. Congress sent Dr. Franklin, Mr. Adams, and Mr. Rutledge, each with his belt of wampum. But finding that his lordship was still harping on the old string, pardons! pardons! they very soon closed the conference.

Towards the close of the trying campaign, it is a fact, that Washington had not 3000 men; and even these were so destitute of necessaries, that nothing but their love and veneration for him kept them together. And with this handful he had to oppose a victorious army, of nearly forty thousand veterans!! But Jehovah, the God of Hosts, was with him: and oft' times, in the ear of the slumbering hero, his voice was heard, "fear not; for I am with thee. Be not dismayed; for I am thy God."—Hence under all the disheartening circumstances of this campaign, Washington not only kept up his own spirits, but cheered those of his drooping comrades. Hearing his officers one day talk about the gloominess of the American affairs, he humorously clasped his neck with his hands, and said with a smile, "I really cannot believe yet, that my neck was ever made for a halter!"

For four months during the summer and fall of 1776, the Americans were obliged to retreat before the enemy, who completely over-ran the Jerseys, filling every town and hamlet with their victorious troops—During their pursuit through the Jerseys, the behaviour of the Hessians towards the country people was barbarous in the extreme. To make them fight the better, it seems that they had been told that the Americans, against whom they were warring, were not (like the Europeans) Christians and gentlemen, but mere savages, a race of Cannibals, who would not only tomahawk a poor Hessian, and haul off his hide for a drum's head, but would just as leave barbacue and eat him as they would a pig. "Vat! Vat!" cried the Waldeckers, with eyes staring wild and big as billiard balls, "Vat! eat Hessian man up like vuu hog! Oh mine God and Vader! vot peoples ever been heard of eat Christian man before! Vy! shure, des Mericans must be de deble."

This was Hessian logic: and it inspired them with the utmost abhorrence of the Americans, to whom they thought the worst treatment much too good—they burnt houses—destroyed furniture—killed the stock—abused the women! and spread consternation and ruin along all their march.

To save their families from such horrid tragedies, the Americans flocked in by thousands to general Howe, to take the oath of allegiance. And the best judges were of opinion, that this alarming apostacy would soon become general throughout the two great states of Pennsylvania and New-Jersey! And indeed no wonder; for to most people it appeared that the cause of liberty was a gone cause. But, still firm as the iron rudder-bands that maintain the course of the ship in her trembling flight over raging seas, so firmly did Washington cleave to his countrymen, and cover their retreat.

They had been obliged to retreat from Long-Island to New-York, from New-York, over the Hudson, to New-Jersey, and now over the Delaware, to Pennsylvania. "My God!" general Washington, "how long shall we retreat?" said general Reed, "where shall we stop?" "Why sir," replied Washington, "if we can do no better, we'll retreat over every river in America; and last of all over the mountains, whence we shall never lack opportunities to annoy, and finally, I hope, to expel the enemies of our country."

But, God be thanked, our toils and trials were not to be pushed to such sad extremities: for general Howe, having driven the Americans to the western side of the Delaware, stationed 4000 men in Trenton, Bordentown, and Burlington, on its eastern bank; and then returned with the main army to eat their winter puddings in Brunswick and New-York. Here Washington, with joy, first discovered an opportunity to make a blow. Not doubting, but that such a long run of success had taught the enemy to think very highly of themselves, and as meanly of the Americans; and suspecting, too, that at Christmas, which was close at hand, instead of watching and praying like good Christians, they would, very likely, be drinking and hopping like fools, he determined then and there if possible to break up their winter quarters. To this end he broke his little remnant of an army into three divisions; two of which he committed to Generals Ewing and Cadwallader to attack at Bordentown and Burlington. The third he meant to lead in person to the heavier charge on Trenton. Every thing being in readiness by Christmas night, as soon as it was dark, they struck their tents, and moved off in high spirits, once more to try their fortune against an enemy long victorious. But alas! the enthusiasm of the gallant Cadwallader and Ewing was soon arrested; for on arriving at the river, they found it so filled with ice, as to preclude all possibility of crossing. Thus, to their inexpressible grief, was blasted the ardent wish to aid their beloved chief in this his last bold attempt to save America. Ignorant of the failure of two-thirds of his plan, Washington and his little forlorn hope, pressed on through the darksome night, pelted by an incessant storm of hail and snow. On approaching the river, nine miles above Trenton, they heard the unwelcome roar of ice, loud crashing along the angry flood. But the object before them was too vast to allow one thought about difficulties. The troops were instantly embarked, and after five hours of infinite toil and danger, landed, some of them frostbitten, on the same shores with the enemy. Forming the line, they renewed their march. Pale, and slowly moving along the neighbouring hills was seen, (by Fancy's eye) the weeping genius of liberty. Driven from the rest of the world, she had fled to the wild woods of America, as to an assured asylum of rest.———Here she fondly hoped, through long unfailing time, to see her children pursuing their cheerful toils, unstarved and uncrushed by the inhuman few. But alas! the inhuman few, with fleets and armies, had pursued her flight! Her sons had gathered around her, but they had failed—some, on their bloody beds; others dispersed; all desponding. One little band alone remained! and, now, resolved to defend her or perish, were in rapid march to face her foes. Pale and in tears, with eyes often lifted to Heaven, she moved along with her children to witness perhaps the last conflict.

The Sun had just tipped with gold the adjacent hills, when snowy Trenton, with the wide-tented fields of the foe, hove in sight. To the young in arms this was an awful scene: and Nature called a short-lived terror to their hearts. But not unseen of Washington was their fear. He marked the sudden paleness of their cheeks, when first they beheld the enemy, and quick, with half-stifled sighs, turned on him their wistful looks. As the big lion of Zara, calling his brindled sons to battle against the mighty rhinoceros, if he mark their falling manes, and sees them crouching to his side, instantly puts on all his terrors—his eyes roll in blood—he shakes the forest with the deepening roar, till, kindled by their father's fire, the maddening cubs swell with answering rage, and spring undaunted on the monster. Thus stately and terrible rode Columbia's first and greatest son, along the front of his halting troops. The eager wish for battle flushed over his burning face, as, rising on his stirrups, he waved his sword towards the hostile camp, and exclaimed, "There! my brave friends! there are the enemies of your country! and now, all I ask of you, is, just to remember what you are about to fight for. March!" His looks and voice rekindled all their fire, and drove them undaunted to the charge. The enemy saw their danger when it was too late! but, as if resolved by taxing their courage, to pay for their carelessness, they roused the thunder of their drums, and flew to arms. But

before they could form, the Americans, led on by
Washington, advanced upon them in a stream of
lightning, which soon decided the contest. By the
musket of the intrepid captain (now General) Freling-
huysen, of New Jersey, fell Col. Rahl, a brave German who commanded the enemy. The ghosts of forty
of his countrymen accompanied him; and very nearly
one thousand were made prisoners. Five hundred
British horse effected their escape to Bordentown.
Could Ewing and Cadwallader have crossed the
river, agreeably to Washington's plan, the enemy's
whole line of cantonments would have been com
pletely swept!!

To rouse his desponding countrymen Washington
immediately marched down to Philadelphia, and
made triumphal entry with his prisoners, preceded
by their cannon and colours, and wagons, bristling
with muskets and bayonets. The poor tories could
scarcely believe their own eyes. Many of the whigs
wept for joy.

To remove from the minds of the Hessians, their
ill-grounded dread of the Americans, Washington
took great care, from the moment they fell into his
hands, to have them treated with the utmost tenderness
and generosity. He contrived that the wealthy Dutch
farmers should come in from the country and converse
with them. They seemed very agreeably surprised
at such friendly attentions. The Dutchmen at length
proposed to them to quit the British service and
become farmers.—At this the Hessians paused a little,
and said something about parting with their country.

" Your country !" said the farmers. " Poor fellows ! where is your country? You have no country.
To support his pomps and pleasures your prince has
torn you from your country, and for 30l. a-head sold
you like slaves to fight against us, who never
troubled you. Then leave the vile employment and
come live with us. Our lands are rich. Come help
us to cultivate them. Our tables are covered with

fat meats, and with milk and honey. Come sit down and eat with us like brothers. Our daughters are young and beautiful and good. Then shew yourselves worthy, and you shall have our daughters: and we will give you of our lands and cattle, that you may work, and become rich and happy as we are. You were told that General Washington and the Americans were savages and would devour you! But from the moment you threw down your arms, have they not been as kind to you as you had any right to expect ?"

"O yes !" cried they, "and a thousand times more kind than we deserved. We were told the Americans would show us no pity, and so we were cruel to them. But we are sorry for it now, since they have been so good to us : and now we love the Americans, and will never fight against them any more !"

Such was the effect of Washington's policy; the divine policy of doing good for evil. It melted down his iron enemies into golden friends. It caused the Hessian soldiers to join with the American farmers ! —not only so, but to write such letters to their countrymen, that they were constantly breaking loose from the British to run over to the Americans —insomuch that in a little time the British would hardly trust a Hessian to stand sentinel !

Though this victory was gained on the 26th of December, yet we find Washington again, on the 1st of January, across the angry Delaware, with his country's flag bold waving over the heights of Trenton. Lord Cornwallis advanced in great force to attack him. The Americans retreated through the town, and crossing the Sanpink (a creek that runs along its eastern side,) planted their cannon near the ford, to defend its passage. The British army following, close in their rear, entered the town about four o'clock ; and a heavy cannonade commenced between the two armies, which were separated only by the Sanpink and its narrow valley. "Now, sir!" said Sir William Erskine to Cornwallis, "now is the time to make sure of Washington.

"Oh no!" replied Cornwallis, "our troops have marched a good way to-day and are tired. And the old fox can't make his escape; for, with the help of the Delaware now filled up with ice, we have completely surrounded him. To-morrow morning, fresh and fasting we'll fall upon him, and take him and his ragamuffins all at once!"

"Ah! my Lord!" returned Sir William, "if Washington be the soldier that I fear he is, you'll not see him there to-morrow morning!"

Night coming on, the artillery ceased to roar; and lighting up their fires, both armies proceeded to supper and to sleep. About midnight, having renewed all the fires, Washington put his little army in motion, and passing along the enemy's rear, hasted to surprise a large body of their troops at Princeton. Soon as it was day Cornwallis was greatly mortified to find there was no American army on the banks of the Sanpink. "That's exactly what I feared," said Sir William. Just as they were in deep thought on the matter, they heard the roar of Washington's cannon at Princeton. "There," continued Sir William, "There is Washington now, cutting up our troops." And so it was; for on arriving at Princeton, about sunrise, Washington met three British regiments, who had just struck their tents, and were coming on in high spirits to attack him at Trenton. In a moment, both parties attacked like heroes. At the first onset the Americans gave way; but sensible that all was at stake, Washington snatched a standard, and advancing on the enemy, called to his countrymen to follow : his countrymen heard, and rushed on to the charge. Then flash and clash went the muskets and bayonets. Here the servants of George, and there the sons of liberty, wrapped in clouds and flames, and inflicting mutual wounds.

9

"God save the king!" the British heroes cried.
"And God for Washington!" Columbia's sons replied.

The name of Washington imparted its usual
animation to his troops. The enemy gave way in
all quarters, and were pursued four miles. The
victors returned with 400 prisoners; the bayonet had
stopped 120 on the field. But they fell not alone
The gallant Mercer, and sixty-three of his brave
countrymen sleep with them. But the strife of the
heroes was but for a moment; and they have forgotten their wounds. Together now, they feast in
Paradise, and when meet their eyes of love, their
joys are not dashed by the remembrance of the
past.

The British officers gave Washington full credit
for such fine strokes of generalship, and began to
look thoughtful whenever his name was mentioned.

The enemy on the 15th of January drew in all
their forces to winter-quarters at Brunswick, where
Washington continued to thin their numbers by cutting off their foraging parties; so that every load of
hay, or dish of turnips they get, was at the price of
their lives.

Thus gloriously, in ten days, was turned the tide
of victory in favour of America, by him whom
Heaven, in mercy not to America alone, but to
Britain, and to the world, had raised up to found
here a wide empire of liberty and virtue. The
character of Washington was exalted to the highest
pitch, even throughout Europe, where he was generally styled the American Fabius, from the famous
Roman general of that name, who opposed Hannibal
with success. A distinction to which he was justly
entitled, from the invincible firmness with which he
rejected every finesse of the British generals; as
also, that admirable judgment with which he suited
the defence of the nation to the genius and abilities
of the people, and to the natural advantages of the

country, thereby not allowing the enemy to pront by their great superiority of numbers, discipline, and artillery, and constantly cutting them off by skirmishes and surprise.

The ministerial plan for 1777, was to reduce the Americans, by intercepting all communications between the northern and southern states! To effect this object General Howe, with 20 thousand men, was to go round from New York to the Head of Elk, and thence march on, due north, through Philadelphia; while General Burgoyne, with 10,000 men, setting out from Canada, was to pass down the lakes, and thence due south to meet his colleague Howe; the straight line, formed by the junction of these two gentlemen, was to possess such virtues, that it was supposed no American could be found hardy enough to set foot over it!!

Accordingly, July 23, General Howe left Sandy Hook; sailed up the Chesapeake; landed at the mouth of Elk River; and with but little interruption, except at Brandywine, marched on to Philadelphia. Into that elegant city, on the 26th of September, 1777, he entered in triumph; fondly supposing, that, in America, as in Europe, the capture of the city was equivalent to the reduction of the country. But instead of finding himself master of this great continent, whose rattle-snakes alone in the hand of heaven, could scourge his presumption; it was with no small difficulty he could keep possession of the little village of Germantown. For, on the morning of the 4th of October, Washington made an attack on him with such judgment and fury, that his troops gave way in every quarter. "The tumult, disorder and despair in the British army," says Washington, "were unparalleled." But in the very moment of the most decisive and glorious victory, when some of the provincial regiments had more prisoners than men, the Americans, through the mistake of an officer, who had drank too freely, began to retreat!!

Washington's grief and mortification were inexpressible.

But while he was annoying the enemy by land, he
did not lose sight of their fleet, which was now forcing its way up the Delaware, to keep open to the
army a channel of supplies. They arrived, without
molestation, within 8 miles of Philadelphia, at a
marsh called Mud-Island. On this poor harmless
spot, the fittest, however, that nature in this peaceful
land of Friends could furnish, Washington ordered a
fort to be thrown up, the command of which, with
230 men, he assigned to lieutenant-colonel Samuel
Smith. On the eastern or Jersey side of the river, at
a place called Red-Bank, he ordered a strong redoubt,
the command of which, with 250 men, was given to
Colonel Greene. These, with some chevaux-de-frise
sunk in the river, and a few gallies, formed all the
barrier that Washington could present against the
British navy. The strength of this barrier was soon
put to a fiery trial. Great preparations were made
to attack the Americans, at the same instant, both by
land and water. Count Donop, with a host of Hessians, was sent over to be in readiness to attack Red-
Bank, while the flood-tide, groaning under the enormous weight, brought up the men of war. The
morning was still, and the heavens overcast with sad
clouds, as of nature sympathizing with her children,
and ready to drop showers of celestial pity on their
strifes. No sooner had the ships floated up within
three cables length of the fort, than they began a most
tremendous cannonade : while cannon-balls and fire-
tailed bombs, like comets, fell upon it thick as hail.
The gallant Smith and his myrmidons stood the shock
to a miracle : and, like men fighting under the eye of
their Washington, drove two-and-thirty pounders
through them with such spirit and success, that in a
little time, the Augusta, a heavy 64 gun ship, took
fire, and blew up, the horrible balloon of many of the
crew. Another ship called the Merlin, or Black-Bird,

soon got on the wing, blew up likewise, and went off in thunder to join the Augusta.

At the same moment Col. Donop, with his Hessians, made a gallant attack on the fort at Red-Bank After a few well-directed fires, Greene and his men artfully retired from the out-works. The enemy now supposing the day their own, rushed on in vast numbers along a large opening in the fort, and within twenty steps of a masked battery, of 18 pounders, loaded with grape-shot and spike-nails. All at once Erebus seemed to open before their affrighted view. But their pains and their terrors were but for a moment. Together down they sunk by hundreds, into the sweet slumbers of death, scarcely sensible of the fatal blow that reft their lives

> Heaps on heaps the slaughter'd Hessians lie :
> Brave Greene beholds them with a tearful eye.
> Far now from home, and from their native shore,
> They sleep in death, and hear of wars no more.

Poor Donop was mortally wounded, and taken prisoner. The attentions of the American officers, and particularly the kind condolence of the godlike Washington, quite overcame him; and his last moments were steeped in tears of regret, for having left his native land to fight a distant people who had never injured him.

On hearing of his misfortune, Washington sent an officer to condole with him. The officer was conducted to his apartment; and delivered the message. The wounded count appeared much affected—a tear swelled in his eye: and he said to the officer, "Present to General Washington the thanks of an unfortunate brother soldier: tell him I expect to rise no more, but if I should, the first exertion of my strength shall be, to return to him my thanks in person." The officer sent was Colonel Daniel Clymer, of Berks, Pennsylvania. "See here, Colonel," said the dying count, "see in me the vanity of all human pride! I

g*

have shone in all the courts of Europe; and now I
am dying here, on the banks of the Delaware, in the
house of an obscure Quaker!"

After six weeks of infinite fatigue, with great loss
of men and money, the British forced a passage large
enough for their provision ships to Philadelphia,
where General Howe and his officers held their balls
this winter; while 16 miles distant, the great Washington, well pleased with his campaign, retired to
winter quarters at Valley Forge.

While such ill success attended this part of the
ministerial plan, viz. to choke the colonies by a military noose, so tightly drawn from Chesapeake to
Champlain, as to stop all circulation between the
northern and southern states; a worse fate frowned
on their attempt in the north. General Burgoyne,
with 10,000 veterans, besides a host of Canadians
and Indians, issuing forth from Canada in June 1777,
came pouring along down the lakes like the thundering Niagara, with an impetuosity that swept every
thing before it. The hatchets of the Indians were
drunk with American blood. No age, no sex, could
soften them. "The widow's wail, the virgin's shriek,
and trembling infant's cry," were music in their ears.
In cold blood they struck their cruel tomahawks into
the defenceless heart of a Miss M'Rea, a beautiful
girl, who was that very day to have been married!
Such acts of inhumanity called forth the fiercest
indignation of the Americans, and inspired that desperate resolution of which the human heart is capable, but which no human force can conquer. The
New Englanders, who were nearest to these infernal
scenes, turned out en masse. Washington hurried
on Gates and Arnold with their furious legions; and
to these he joined the immortal Morgan with his
dreadful phalanx, 1000 riflemen, whose triggers were
never touched in vain, but could throw a ball a
hundred yards at a squirrel's head, and never miss.

The first check given to Burgoyne's career, was at

Bennington. Hearing that the Americans had laid up large provisions in that town, he detached a Colonel Baum, with 600 Germans, to surprise it: and, at the same time, posted Colonel Breyman in the neighbourhood, with an equal number to support him if necessary. Finding the place too well guarded either for surprise or storm, Baum fortified himself at a little distance, and sent back for Breyman. The American commander, the brave General Starke, sallied out, and with great fury attacked Baum's intrenchments without giving him time to receive his reinforcements. At the first onset, the Canadians and British marksmen took to their heels, and left the poor Germans in the lurch. After a gallant resistance, Baum was mortally wounded, and his brave countrymen killed or taken to a man. In the meantime Breyman, totally ignorant of their catastrophe, arrived at the place of action, where, instead of the cheering huzzas of joyful friends, he was saluted, on all hands, with the deadly whizzing of rifle bullets. After receiving a few close and scorching fires, the Germans hastily betook themselves to flight. The neighbouring woods, with night's sable curtains, enabled the fugitives to save themselves for that time at least. The enemy lost in these two engagements, not less than 1000 men, killed, wounded, and prisoners.

About the same time all their forts on the lakes were surprised. Colonel St. Leger was defeated at Fort-Stanwix; the Indians began to desert; Arnold and Morgan were coming up like mountain-storms: and the militia from all quarters were pouring in. Burgoyne began to be alarmed, and wrote to New York for aid; but finding that Clinton could give him none, and that the salvation of his army depended on themselves, he gallantly determined, on the 7th of October, 1777, to stake his all on the issue of a general battle.

His army, in high spirits, was formed within a mile of the American camp. Burgoyne, with the flower of the British troops, composed the centre. Brigá dier-general Frazer commanded the left. The Germans, headed by major-generals Philips and Reidesdel, and col. Breyman formed the right. With a fine train of artillery, flying colours, and full roll of martial music, from wing to wing the towering heroes moved. On the other hand, fired with the love of liberty, the Americans poured out by thousands, eager for the glorious contest. Their dear country's flag waves over their heads. The thoughts of the warriors are on their children, and on the chains now forging for their tender hands. The avenging passions rise, and the battle moves. Morgan brought on the action. In a large buckwheat field, which lay between the two armies, he had concealed his famous regiment of riflemen. The enemies, chiefly Canadians and Indians, unsuspiciously advance. They were suffered to come within point blank shot, when they received a general fire, which strewed the field with their dead bodies. Morgan pursued; but was soon met by a heavy reinforcement from the British, who quickly drove him, in turn. Arnold then moved on to support Morgan; and, in a short time, with nine heavy regiments was closely engaged with the whole of the British army, both parties fighting as if each was determined never to yield: while the incessant crash of muskets and roar of artillery appeared both to sight and sound as if two wrathful clouds had come down on the plain, rushing together, in hideous battle, with all their thunders and lightnings. The weight, however, of the American fire was directed against the enemy's centre, extending along the left wing: and though it was some time sustained with the greatest firmness, yet at length it prevailed, and threw the British into confusion. But the gallant Frazer flying to their assistance, soon restored their order and renewed the fight. Severely galled still by Morgan's rifles on the flanks, and hard pressed at the same time, in front by Arnold, they gave way a

second time ; and a second time Frazer's presence
revived their valour, and rekindled the battle in all
its rage.

Here Arnold did an act unworthy of the glory of
the well fought battle. He ordered up twelve of his
best riflemen, and pointing to Frazer, who on horseback, with brandished sword, was gallantly animating his men, he said : " Mark that officer !—Himself
is a host ; let me not see him long."

The riflemen flew to their places, and in a few
moments the hero was cut down. With him fell the
courage of the left wing, who, being now fiercely
charged, gave way, and retreated to their camp. But
scarcely had they entered it, when the Americans,
with Arnold at their head, stormed it with inconceiv-
able fury; rushing with trailed arms through a heavy
discharge of musketry and grape shot. The British
fought with equal desperation. For their all was at
stake; the Americans, like a whelming flood, were
bursting over their intrenchments ; and, hand to hand,
with arguments of bloody steel, were pleading the
cause of ages yet unborn. Hoarse as a mastiff of true
British breed, Lord Balcarras was heard from rank to
rank, loud-animating his troops; while on the other
hand, fierce as the hungry tiger of Bengal, the impetuous Arnold precipitated his heroes on the stubborn
foe. High in air, the encountering banners blazed ;
there bold waving the lion-painted standard of Britain ; here the streaming pride of Columbia's lovely
stripes—while thick below, ten thousand eager warriors close the darkening files, all bristled with venge-
ful steel. No firing is heard. But shrill and terrible,
from rank to rank, resounds the clash of bayonets—
frequent and sad the groans of the dying. Pairs on
pairs, Britons and Americans, with each his bayonet
in his brother's breast, fall forward together faint-
shrieking in death, and mingle their smoking blood.

Many were the widows, many the orphans that
were made that day. Long did the daughters of

Columb.a mourn their fallen brothers! and often.did the lovely maids of Caledonia roll their soft blue eyes of sorrow along the sky-bound sea, to meet the sails of their returning lovers.

But alas! their lovers shall return no more. Far distant, on the banks of the roaring Hudson they lie, pale and helpless on the fields of death. Glassy now and dim are those eyes which once " beamed with friendship, or which flamed in war." Their last thoughts are towards the maids of their love: and the big tears glisten in their eye, as they heave the parting groan.

Then was seen the faded form of Ocean's Queen. far-famed Britannia, sitting alone and tearful on her western cliff. With downcast look her faithful lion lay roaring at her feet; while torn and scattered on the rock were seen her many trophies of ancient fame. Silent, in dishevelled locks, the goddess sat, absorbed in grief, when the gale of the west came blackening along the wave, laden with the roar of murderous battle. At once she rose—a livid horror bespread her cheeks—distraction glared on her eyeballs, hard strained towards the place whence came the groans of her children! the groans of her children fast sinking in a distant land. Thrice she essayed to curse the destroyers of her race. But thrice she remembered, that they too were her sons. Then, wild shrieking with a mother's anguish, she rent the air with her cries: and the hated name of North resounded through all her caves.

But still in all its rage the battle burned: and both parties fought with an obstinacy, never exceeded. But, in that moment of danger and of glory, the impetuous Arnold, who led the Americans, was dangerously wounded, and forced to retire; and several regiments of British infantry pouring in to the assistance of their gallant comrades, the Americans, after many hard struggles, were finally repulsed.

∴ In another quarter, where the strength of the Germans fought, the Americans, led on by Morgan, carried the intrenchments sword in hand. The face of Morgan was like the full moon in a stormy night, when she looks down red and fiery on the raging deep, amidst foundering wrecks and cries of drowning seamen; while his voice, like thunder on the hills, was heard, loud-shouting his heroes to the bloody charge. The tall regiments of Hesse Cassel fell or fled before them; leaving their baggage, tents and artillery, in the hands of the victors.

This was a bloody day to both armies: but so peculiarly disheartening to the British, that they were obliged to retreat that night to Saratoga, where, in a few days, (on the 13th of October, 1777,) they surrendered to the Americans, under Gates, by whom they were treated with a generosity that astonished them. For, when the British were marched out to lay down their arms, there was not an American to be seen! They had all nobly retired for a moment, as if unwilling to give the pain, even to their enemies, of being spectators of so humiliating a scene! Worthy countrymen of Washington! this deed of yours shall outlive the stars, and the blest sun himself, smiling, shall proclaim, that in the wide travel of his beams, he never looked upon its like before.

Thus, gloriously for America, ended the campaign of '77. That of '78 began as auspiciously. In May, Silas Deane arrived from France, with the welcome news of a treaty with that powerful people, and a letter from Louis XVI. to Congress, whom he styled —very dear great friends and allies.

Soon as it was known by the British ambassador at Paris, Lord Stormont, that the king of France had taken part with the Americans, he waited on the French minister, De Vergennes; and with great agitation mentioned the report, asking if it were possible it could be true.

"Very possible, my Lord," replied the smooth Frenchman.

"Well, I'm astonished at it, sir," continued Stormont, exceedingly mortified. "America, sir, is our daughter! and it was extremely indelicate of the French king thus to decoy her from our embraces, and make a w——e of her!"

"Why as to that matter, my Lord," quoth Vergennes, with the true Gallic shrug, "there is no great harm done. For the king of France is very willing to marry your daughter, and make an honest woman of her.

CHAPTER X.

Lord North, coming to his senses, sends commissioners to America—Clinton evacuates Philadelphia—Washington pursues him—battle of Monmouth—Arnold's apostacy—Andre apprehended—executed—his character

THE news of the total loss of Burgoyne and his army soon reached Parliament, where it produced a consternation never before known in that house. The Ministry, utterly confounded, could not open their lips; while the Whig minority, with great severity, lashed their obstinacy and ignorance. Lord North, beginning now to find, as the great Chatham had foretold, that "three millions of Whigs, with arms in their hands, were not to be enslaved," became very anxious to conciliate! Commissioners were sent over with offers to repeal the abnoxious taxes! and also with promises of great favours which Lord North would confer on America, if she would settle the dispute with the mother country. The better to dispose her towards these offers, elegant presents were to be made to her best friends, (such as Washington, the President of Congress, &c. &c.,)

to speak a good word for Lord North's favours!!
But, observe, Independence was to be out of the
question.

Doctor Franklin used laughingly to say, that "Lord
North and his great favours, put him in mind of an
old bawd, and her attempts upon a young virgin, to
whom she promised every thing but Innocence.
While in robbing her of innocence, the old hag knew
well enough that she was robbing the poor girl of
that without which she would soon, in spite of her
fine gowns and necklaces, become a miserable out-
cast and slave "

Finding that Lord North, in the multitude of his
favours, had entirely forgotten the only one which
they valued, i. e. the Independence of their country,
the committee of Congress broke off all farther converse with the ministerial commissioners, who proceeded immediately to try the efficacy of their
presents. To Washington, 'tis said, a viceroyship,
with tons of gold, was to have been tendered. But,
to the honour of the commissioners be it said, not
one of their number was graceless enough to breathe
the polluted wish into his ear. They had, however,
the hardihood to throw out a bait of 10,000 guineas
to the President of Congress, Gen. Reed. His
answer is worthy of lasting remembrance. "Gentlemen," said he, "I am poor, very poor. But your
king is not rich enough to buy me !"

On the 18th of June, the British army, now under
the command of Clinton, evacuated Philadelphia for
New York. The figure they made on the road had
something of the air of the sublime ; for their baggage, loaded horses, and carriages, formed a line not
less than twelve miles in length. General Washington, whose eye, like that of the sacred dragon, was
always open, and fixed upon the enemies of America,
immediately crossed the Delaware after them—
pushed on detached corps to obstruct their advance
—gall their flanks—and fall on their rear, while he

10

himself moved on with the main body of the army.
By the 27th, Clinton had advanced as far as Monmouth : and Washington's troops were close on his
flank and rear. Next morning Gen. Lee, with 5000
men, was ordered to begin the attack ; Washington
moving on briskly to support him. But, as he
advanced, to his infinite astonishment he met Lee
retreating, and the enemy pursuing. "For God's
sake, General Lee," said Washington with great
warmth, "what's the cause of this ill-tim'd prudence ?"

"No man, sir," replied Lee, quite convulsed with
rage, "can boast a larger portion of that rascally
virtue than your Excellency ! !"

Dashing along by the madman, Washington rode
up to his troops, who, at sight of him, rent the air
with "God save great Washington !"

"My brave fellows," said he, "can you fight ?"

They answered with three cheers ! "Then face
about, my heroes, and charge."—This order was
executed with infinite spirit. The enemy, finding
themselves now warmly opposed in front, made an
attempt to turn his left flank ; but were gallantly
attacked and driven back. They then made a rapid
push to the right : but the brave Greene, with a
choice body of troops and artillery, repulsed them
with considerable slaughter. At the same instant,
Wayne advanced with his legion ; and poured in so
severe and well directed a fire, that the enemy were
glad to regain their defiles. Morgan's rifles distinguished themselves that day. Washington and his
heroes lay upon their arms all night, resolved to fall
on the enemy the moment they should attempt their
retreat next morning. But during the night, they
moved off in silence ; and got such a start, that
Washington thought it dangerous, in such hot
weather, to make a push after them. The Americans lost 58 killed—140 wounded. The British had
349 killed, and the wounded in proportion. Numbers,

on both sides, died of the extreme heat, and by drinking cold water.

In September 1780, an attempt was made to take
off our Washington, and by means which I can hardly believe the old British lion was ever well pleased
with.

I allude to the affair of Arnold's treason. That
which makes rogues of thousands, I mean Extravagance, was the ruin of this great soldier. Though
extremely brave, he was of that vulgar sort, who
having no taste for the pleasures of the mind, think
of nothing but high living, dress, and show. To rent
large houses in Philadelphia—to entertain French
Ambassadors—to give balls and concerts, and grand
dinners and suppers—required more money than he
could honestly command. And, alas! such is the
stuff whereof spendthrifts are made, that to fatten
his Prodigality, Arnold consented to starve his Honesty: and provided he might but figure as a gorgeous Governor, he was content to retail, by the billet
and the gill, wood and rum unfairly drawn from the
commissary's store!

Colonel Melcher, the barrack master, mentioned
the matter to Congress, who desired him to issue to
General Arnold no more than his proper rations. He
had scarcely returned home when Arnold's servant
appeared with an order for another large supply of
Rum, Hickory wood, &c. &c.

"Inform your master," said Melcher, "that he
can't have so much."

Arnold immediately came down; and in a great
passion asked Colonel Melcher, if it was true he had
protested his bill?

"Yes, sir!"

"And how durst you do it?"

"By order of Congress, sir."

At this, Arnold, half choked with rage, replied,
"D——n the rascals! I'll remember them for it.
Sampson-like I'll shake the pillars of their Liberty
temple about their ears.

On the evacuation of Philadelphia by the British, Gen. Arnold had been appointed temporary governor of that city, where he behaved like a desperado, who hesitates at nothing to stop the deadly leaks of his prodigality, and to keep himself from sinking. Among other bold strokes, he seized and sold large quantities of American property, pretending it was British. Complaints were made to Congress, who, unwilling to expose the man who had fought so gallantly for Liberty, treated him with great gentleness: and for the same reason, Washington, after a mild reproof, gave him the command of West Point, with a large body of troops.

The history of Arnold's embarrassments and his quarrel with his countrymen, soon reached New York. The British commander, well knowing the ticklish situation of a proud man, caught on the horns of poverty, sends up major Andre, with money in his pocket. The major, by means yet unknown to the public, got near enough to Arnold to probe him; and, alas! found him, both in principle and purse, hollow as an exhausted receiver, and very willing to be filled up with English guineas. English guineas, to the tune of ten thousand, with the rank and pay of Brigadier General, are offered him: and Arnold agrees, Oh! shocking to humanity! Arnold agrees to sacrifice Washington.

The outlines of the project were, it seems, that Arnold should make such a disposition of the troops at West Point, as to enable Sir Henry Clinton, so completely to surprise them, that they must inevitably, either lay down their arms or be cut to pieces—with General Washington among them!! The victorious British were then, both by land and water, to rush upon the feeble and dispirited residue of the American army, in the neighbourhood, utterly unable to resist, when there would follow such a slaughter of men, and such a sweeping of artillery, ammunition, stores, &c. &c., as would completely break down the spirit of the nation, and reduce them to unconditional submission to the Ministry!

To be certified of this delightful truth, Andre, during Washington's absence from West Point, comes ashore from a sloop of war, with a surtout over his regimentals; spends a day and night with Arnold; sees with his own eyes, the dear train laid, the matches lighted, and every thing in readiness, a few nights hence, to send the old Virginia farmer and his republic to destruction.

Every thing being settled to satisfaction, Andre wishes to set off to carry the glorious news to General Clinton. But, behold! by a fine stroke of Providential interference, he cannot get on board the ship!! Arnold gives him a horse and a pass to go to New York by land. Under the name of Anderson he passes, in safety, all the guards. Now, like an uncaged bird, and light as the air he breathes, he sweeps along the road. His fame brightens before him— stars and garters, coaches and castles, dance before his delighted fancy—even his long-loved reluctant Delia (Miss Seward) is all his own—she joins in the nation's gratitude—softly she rolls her eyes of love, and brightening in all her beauty, sinks on his enraptured breast! In the midst of these, too, too happy thoughts, he is met by three young militia men. Though not on duty, they challenged him. He answers by the name of Anderson; shews his pass; and bounds away. Here the guardian genius of Columbia burst into tears—she saw the fall of her hero, and her country's liberties crushed for ever. Dry thine eyes, blest saint, thy Washington is not fallen yet. The thick bosses of Jehovah's buckler are before the chief: and the shafts of his enemies shall yet fall to the earth, accurst—For, scarce had Andre passed the young militia-men, before one of them tells his comrades, that "he does not like his looks;" and insists that he shall be called back, and questioned again. His answers prove him a spy:

10*

He would have fled: but they level their muskets.
Trembling and pale, he offers them an elegant gold-
watch to let him go. No! He presses on them a
purse bloated with guineas. No! He promises each
of them a handsome pension for life—but all in vain.
The power that guarded Washington was wroth with
Andre. On searching him they find in his boot, and
in Arnold's own hand-writing, a plan of the whole
conspiracy! Sons of the generous soul, why should
I tell how major Andre died! The place where his
gallows stood is overgrown with weeds—but smiling
angels often visit the spot; and it was bathed with
the tears of his foes.

His candour, on his examination, in some sort ex-
piated his crime. It melted the angel soul of Washington: and the tears of the hero were mingled with
the ink that signed the death-warrant of the hapless
youth. The names of the young men who arrested
poor Andre, were, John Paulding, David Williams,
and Isaac Van Vert. They were at cards under a
large poplar that grew by the road, where the major
was to pass. Congress rewarded them with silver
medals; and settled on each of them $200 annually,
for life.

American writers have recorded a thousand handsome things of unfortunate Andre. They have made
him scholar, soldier, gentleman, poet, painter, musi-
cian, and, in short, every thing that talents and taste
can make a man. The following anecdote will show
that he was much greater still.

Some short time before that fatal affair which
brought him to his end, (said my informant, Mr.
Drewy, a painter, now living at Newbern,) a foraging party from New-York made an inroad into our
settlement near that city. The neighbours soon assembled to oppose them; and, though not above fifteen years old, I turned out with my friends. In company was another boy, in age and size nearly about
my own speed. We had counted on a fine chase.

CAPTURE OF MAJOR ANDRE.

But the British were not to be driven so easily as we had expected. Standing their ground, they not only put us to flight, but captured several of our party; myself and the other boy among them. They presently set out with us for New-York: and, all the way, as we were going, my heart ached to think how my poor mother and sisters would be distressed when night came, and I did not return. Soon as they brought me in sight of the prison, I was struck with horror. The gloomy walls, and frightful guards at the doors, and wretched crowds at the iron windows, together with the thoughts of being locked up there in dark dungeons with disease and death, so overcame me, that I bursted into tears. Instantly a richly dressed officer stepped up, and taking me by the hand, with a look of great tenderness, said, "My dear boy! what makes you cry?" I told him I could not help it when I compared my present sad prospect with the happy one I enjoyed in the morning with my mother and sisters at home. "Well, well, my dear child, (said he) don't cry, don't cry any more." Then turning to the jailor ordered him to stop till he should come back. Though but a boy, yet I was deeply struck with the wonderful difference betwixt this man and the rest around me. He appeared to me like a brother; they like brutes. I asked the jailor who he was. "Why, that's Major Andre, (said he angrily) the adjutant-general of the army; and you may thank your stars that he saw you; for I suppose he is gone to the general to beg you off, as he has done many of your d——d rebel countrymen." In a short time he returned; and with great joy in his countenance called out—" Well, my boys, I've good news, good news for you! The general has given you to me, to dispose of as I choose; and now you are at liberty! So run home to your fond parents, and be good boys; mind what they tell you: say your prayers; love one another; and God Almighty will bless you."

And yet Andre perished, on a gallows, while Ar-

nold, after living to old age, died in his bed!! Shall
we hence infer with Brutus, that "Virtue is but an
empty name?" and that Andre had been good in
vain? God forbid! Goodness and happiness are twins;
Heaven hath joined them together, and Hell cannot
put them asunder. For proof, we need go no further
than to Andre himself—to Andre in prison! Even in
that last and gloomiest scene of his life, we see the
power which virtue has to illuminate the dark, to en-
liven the sad, and to raise her votaries above the terrors of death. In the first moment of his capture,
when vulgar minds are thinking of nothing but self-
preservation, he is thinking of nothing but duty and
generosity. Regardless of himself, he is only anxious
for Arnold. Having by letter advised that wretched
man of his danger, and given him time to escape, he
then gallantly asserts his own real character; and
avows himself "the Adjutant General of the British
army."

The truth is, he had been sent by Gen. Clinton, on
a dirty piece of business for which he was not fit;
and of which he was so heartily ashamed, that he appears to have been willing to atone for it with his life.
Hence to the questions put at his trial, he answered
with a candour which at once surprised and melted
the Court Martial—he answered, with the candour of
a mind which feared its own condemnation more than
that of any human tribunal.—He heard his sentence
of death with perfect indifference; and at the place
of execution behaved like one who had fulfilled the
high duties of son, brother, and man, with constant
attention to a happy immortality. Thus giving the
friends of virtue abundant cause to exclaim:

"Far more true peace the dying Andre felt,
Than Arnold ever knew in prosp'rous guilt."

He, poor wretch, survived! but only to live a life, at
once hated and despised—hated by the British Gene-

al, whom he had shown capable of assassinating the man he could not conquer—hated by the British army, whom he had robbed of one of its brightest ornaments—and hated by the officers, who could not bear to see what they called "a d—mn'd trator," not only introduced into their company, but placed over their heads? In short, Arnold was an eye-sore *to every man* of honour in England, where he was often most grossly insulted.

Soon after his flight to England with the slender remains of the British army, he went down to Southampton, where the broken-hearted Mother and Sisters of the unfortunate Andre lived. And so little was he acquainted with the human heart, that he called to see them! On hearing his name announced by the servant, they burst into tears; and sent him word, that "they did not wish to see him."

The moment he received Major Andre's letter, the terrified Arnold made his escape to New-York.

British historians have wondered that he left his wife in the power of Washington. But Arnold knew in whom he trusted: and the generous man behaved exactly as Arnold had foreseen; for he immediately sent him his clothes and baggage; and wrote a polite letter of condolence to his lady, offering her a conveyance to her husband, or to her friends in Pennsylvania.

Washington now waged the war with various success. On the one hand, his hero of Saratoga (Gates) was defeated with great loss, at Camden; on the other, the British lost, on the King's-Mountain, the brave Colonel Ferguson, with all his army, 1,400 men. Colonel Ferguson and his men were supposed by the British, the most exquisite marksmen alive. And indeed to hear their bravadoes, one would suppose, that give them but guns of a proper calibre, and they would think it a light affair to snuff the moon, or drive the centre of the fixed stars. But the American Rifle-boys soon led them into a truer way of thinking. For in a few rounds they pink'd the

brave Colonel, and put 3000 of his exquisite marksmen asleep; which struck such a wholesome panic
into the survivors, that they threw down their arms,
and like thrifty gentlemen called out right lustily for
quarters.

But few of the Americans fell; but among these
was one, whose fame "Time with his own eternal
lip shall sing." I mean the brave Col. Williams.
He it was, whose burning words first kindled the
young farmers at their ploughs, and led them to the
King's Mountain, to measure their youthful rifles
with Ferguson's heroes. On receiving the ball
which opened in his breast the crimson sluice of life,
he was borne by his aids, into the rear; where he
was scarcely laid down, fainting with loss of blood,
before a voice was heard, loud exclaiming, "Hurra!
my boys! the day is our own! the day is our own!
they are crying for quarters!" Instantly he started
as from the incipient sleep of death; and, opening his
heavy eyes, eagerly called out, "My God! who are
crying for quarters?" "The British! The British!"
replied the powder-blackened riflemen. At this, one
last beam of joy lighted in a smile on his dying face:
then faintly whispering, God be praised! he bowed
his head in everlasting peace.

Joy follow thee, my brother, to his blest presence,
who sent thee, a pillar of fire, to blast the mad efforts
of men fighting against their brethren! On earth thy
fame shall never fail. Children yet unborn shall lisp
the name of Williams. Their cherub lips shall often
talk of him whose patriot eye beheld them, afar off,
smiling on the breast, and with a parent's ardour
hasted to ward from their guiltless heads the curses
of monarchy.

After the defeat of Gates, Washington sent on his
favourite Greene to head the southern army against
the victorious Cornwallis and Tarleton. With
Greene he joined the famous Morgan, whose riflemen
had performed such signal service during the war.

To draw Cornwallis's attention from a blow meditated against the British post at Ninety-Six, Greene detached Morgan to Paulet's river, near the neighbourhood of Cornwallis and Tarleton. Immediately the pride of Tarleton rose. He begged of his friend, lord Rawdon, to obtain for him the permission of the commander in chief to go and attack Morgan. "By heavens, my lord," said he, "I could not desire a finer feather in my cap than Col. Morgan. Such a prisoner would make my fortune." "Ah, Ben," replied Rawdon very coolly, "you had better let the old wagoner alone." As no refusal could satisfy, permission at length was granted him: and he instantly set out. At parting, he said to lord Rawdon with a smile, "My lord, if you will be so obliging as to wait dinner, the day after to-morrow, till four o'clock, Col. Morgan shall be one of your lordship's guests." "Very well, Ben," said the other, "we shall wait. But remember, Morgan was brought up under Washington." Tarleton was followed to battle by about 1000 choice infantry and 250 horse, with two field pieces. To oppose this formidable force, Morgan had but 500 militia, 300 regulars, and 75 horse. His militia were but militia. His regulars were the famous Maryland line led by Howard; men who would have done honour to the plains of Austerlitz. The intrepid Desaix, who turned the tide of war in the bloody strife of Marengo, was only equal to Washington, Col. of the horse. Morgan had no wish to fight. But Tarleton compelled him; for about two hours before day, on the 17th of January, 1781, some of Washington's cavalry came galloping into camp with news that the British were but eight miles off, and would be up by day break. Instantly Morgan called a council of war, composed only of Howard, Washington, and himself. "Well, gentlemen," said he, "what's to be done? shall we fight or fly? shall we leave our friends to our enemies; and burning our meal and bacon, so hardly got, turn out again into the starving woods; or shall we stand by both, and fight like men?"

"No burning! no flying," replied they, "but let's stand, and fight like men?"

"Well then, my brave fellows," said Morgan, "wake up the troops, and prepare for action."

The ground, on which this very memorable battle was fought, was an open pine barren. The militia were drawn up about two hundred yards in front of the regulars, and the horse some small distance in the rear. Just after day break, the British came in sight; and halting within a quarter of a mile of the militia, began to prepare for battle. The sun had just risen, as the enemy, with loud shouts, advanced to the charge. The militia, hardly waiting to give them a distant fire, broke and fled for their horses, which were tied at some distance on the wings of the Maryland line. Tarleton's cavalry pushed hard after the fugitives, and, coming up with them just as they had reached their horses, began to cut them down. Unable to bear that sight, Col. Washington, with his corps, dashed on to their rescue. As if certain of victory, Tarleton's men were all scattered in the chase! Washington's heroes, on the contrary, sensible of the fearful odds against them, advanced close and compact as the Spartan phalanx. Then sudden and terrible the charge was made! Like men fighting, life in hand, all at once they rose high on their stirrups! while in streams of lightning their swords came down, and heads and arms, and caps, and carcasses, distained with spouting gore, rolled fearfully all around. Mournfully from all sides the cries of the wounded were heard, and the hollow groans of the dying.

Agonizing with rage and grief, Tarleton beheld the flight of his boasted victory, and the slaughter of his bravest troops. He flew to reanimate them. He encouraged—he threatened—he stormed and raved. But all in vain. No time was given to rally; for like the heavy ship under crowded canvass, bursting through the waves, so strong and resistless, Washington's squadron went on, hewing down and overthrowing every thing in their way. Confounded by such a fatal charge, the British cavalry could not support it; but broke and fled in the utmost precipitation; while, bending forward over their horses, and waving their blood-stained swords, the loud-shouting Americans pursued. The woods resounded with the noise of their flight.

As when a mammoth suddenly dashes in among a thousand buffaloes, feeding at large on the vast plains of Missouri; all at once the innumerous herd, with wildly rolling eyes, and hideous bellowings, break forth into flight, while, close at their heels, the roaring monster follows. Earth trembles as they fly. Such was the noise in the chase of Tarleton, when the swords of Washington's cavalry pursued his troops from the famous fields of the Cowpens. It was like a peal of thunder, loud roaring at first, but gradually dying on the ear as it rolls away along the distant air.

By this time the British infantry had come up: and, having crossed a little valley, just as they ascended the hill, they found themselves within twenty steps of Howard and his regulars, who received them with a right soldierly welcome, and, taking good aim, poured in a general and deadly fire. A slaughter so entirely unexpected, threw the enemy into confusion. Seeing this wonderful change in the battle, the militia recovered their spirits, and began to form on the right of the regulars. Morgan waving his sword, instantly rode up to them, and with a voice of thunder roared out, "Hurra! my brave fellows, form, form! Old Morgan was never beat in his life—one fire more, my heroes, and the day is our own!" With answering shouts, both regulars and militia then advanced upon the enemy; and, following their fire with the bayonet, instantly decided the conflict. The ground was covered with the dead. The tops of the aged pines shook with the ascending ghosts. With feeble cries and groans, at once they rose, like flocks of snow-white swans when the cold blast strikes them on the lakes of Canada, and sends them on wide-spread wings, far to the south to seek a happier clime.

Washington pursued Tarleton 20 miles! and, during the race, was often so near him, that he could easily have killed him with a pistol shot. But having strictly forbidden his men to fire a pistol that day, he could not resolve to break his own orders. However, there was one of his men who broke them. At one time Washington was 30 or 40 yards ahead of his men. Tarleton observing this, suddenly wheeled with a couple of his dragoons to cut him off. Washington, with more courage than prudence, perhaps, dashed on, and rising on his stirrups, made a blow at Tarleton, with such force, that it beat down his guard and mutilated one or two of his fingers. In this unprotected state, one of the British dragoons was aiming a stroke which must have killed him. But the good genii, who guard the name of Washington, prevailed: for in that critical moment a mere dwarf of a Frenchman rushed up, and with a pistol ball shivered the arm of the Briton. The other dragoon attempted to wheel off; but was cut down. Tarleton made his escape.

Tarleton was brave, but not generous. He could not bear to hear another's praise. When some ladies in Charleston were speaking very handsomely of Washington, he replied with a scornful air, that, "He would be very glad to get a sight of Col. Washington. He had heard much talk of him," he said, "but had never seen him yet." "Why, sir," rejoined one of the ladies, "if you had looked behind you at the battle of the Cowpens, you might easily have enjoyed that pleasure."

While in the neighbourhood of Halifax, North

Carolina, Tarleton dined in a large company. The elegant and witty Mrs. Wiley Jones happened to be of the party. The ladies, who were chiefly whigs, were frequently praising the brave Col. Washington. Tarleton with looks considerably angry, replied, "that he was very much surprised that the Americans should think so highly of Col. Washington; for, from what he could learn, he was quite an illiterate fellow and could hardly write his own name." "That may be very true (replied Mrs. Jones) "but I believe, sir you can testify that he "knows how to make his mark." Poor Tarleton looked at his crippled finger, and bit his lips with rage.

General Washington continued the war against the British till 1781; when Cornwallis pushed into Virginia, and fortified himself at York-Town. But the eye of Washington was upon him; and with an address, which, the British historians say, was never equalled, he concerted a plan that ended in the total destruction of Cornwallis. He artfully wrote letters to Greene, informing him, that, " in order to relieve Virginia, he was determined immediately to attack New York." These letters were so disposed as to fall into the right hands. Clinton took the alarm. But while the British general was in daily expectation of a visit from him, Washington and his army, were now across the Delaware, with full stretch to the south, darkening the day with their clouds of rolling dust. Cornwallis saw that the day of his fall was at hand. He had done all that a brave (would to God we could add, a humane) man could do; but all in vain. On the last day of September, Washington sat down before York, with 100 pieces of heavy artillery. On the 7th of October this dreadful train began to thunder: and the British works sunk before them. Lord Cornwallis, unwilling to expose his army to the destruction of a general assault, agreed on the 17th to surrender. This was justly considered the close of the war; which having been begun with

11*

supplication, Washington piously ordered to be finished with thanksgiving.

In the siege of Yorktown, the behaviour of the Americans was, as usual, generous and noble. The amiable Col. Scammel, adjutant-general of the American army, and uncommonly beloved by them, was dangerously wounded and taken prisoner by some British dragoons, who barbarously trotted him on before them, three miles, into town, where he presently died of fever and loss of blood. Great was the mourning for Scammel. In a few nights after, Washington gave orders to storm two of the enemy's redoubts, which were carried almost in an instant. The British called for quarters: A voice of death was heard, "Remember poor Scammel!"—"Remember, gentlemen, you are Americans!" was rejoined by the commander: and instantly the points of the American bayonets were thrown up towards heaven!

The conduct of the French also, was such as to entitle them to equal praise.

For when the British marched out to lay down their arms, the French officers were seen to shed tears. They condoled with the British, and tendered them their purses!—Glorious proof, that God never intended men to be, as some wickedly term it, natural enemies.

On hearing in Congress the fall of Cornwallis, the door-keeper swooned with joy—on hearing the same news announced in parliament, lord North fell back in his chair, in the deepest distress. On receipt of the glad tidings, Congress broke forth into songs of praise to God: Parliament into execrations against their Prime Minister—Congress hastened to the temple to pay their vows to the Most High; the Parliament went to St. James's with a petition to the King for a change of men and measures. The King was graciously pleased to hear the voice of their prayer. Men and measures were changed; and a decree was passed that whoever should advise war

SURRENDER OF LORD CORNWALLIS.

and a farther widening of the breach between Britain
and America, should be denounced an equal enemy
to both.   Then full leafed and green the olive branch
of peace was held out to the nations : and the eyes of
millions, on both sides of the water, were lifted in
transport to the lovely sign.   The stern features of
war were relaxed ; and gladdening smiles began
again to brighten over the " human face divine."
But Washington beheld the lovely sight with doubt.
Long accustomed unerringly to predict what Britain
would do, from what he knew she had power to do,
he had nothing to hope, but every thing to fear.
America, without money or credit !—her officers,
without a dollar in their pocket, strolling about camps
in long beards and dirty shirts—her soldiers often
without a crust in their knapsacks or a dram in their
canteens—and her citizens every where sick and tired
of war !--Great Britain, on the other hand, every where
victorious over the fleets of her enemies—completely
mistress of the watery world, and Judas-like, bag-
bearer of its commerce and cash ! with such resources,
with all these trumps in her hands, she will play
quits, and make a drawn game of it ? Impossible !
but if she should, " it must be the work of that Providence who ruleth in the armies of Heaven and earth,
and whose hand has been visibly displayed in every
step of our progress to independence."   " Nothing,"
continued Washington, " can remove my doubts but
an order from the ministry to remove their fleets and
armies."

That welcome order, at length, was given ! and
the British troops, sprucely powdered and perfumed,
in eager thousands hied on board their ships.

" All hands unmoor !" the stamping boatswain cried :
" All hands unmoor !" the joyous crew replied.

Then in a moment they all fly to work. Some
seizing the ready handspikes, vault high upon the
windlasses ; thence coming down all at once with the

hearty Yo-heave-O, they shake the sounding decks,
and tear from their dark oozy beds the ponderous
anchors. Others, with halyards hard strained through
the creaking blocks, sway aloft the wide-extended
yards, and spread their canvas to the gale, which,
with increasing freshness, bears the broad-winged
ships in foam and thunder through the waves. Great
was the joy of the multitude; for they were hasten-
ing to revisit their native land, and to meet those
eyes of love which create a heaven in a virtuous
breast. But the souls of some were sad. These were
the reflecting few, whose thoughts were on the better
hopes of former days! To them, the flowing bowl,
the lively joke, the hearty laugh and song, gave no
delight; nor yet the blue fields of ocean brightly
shining round, with all her young billows wantoning
before the playful breeze. Their country ruined, and
themselves repulsed, how could they rejoice! Then
slowly retiring from the noisy crew, by themselves
apart they sat on the lofty stern, high above the
burning track which the ships left behind them in
their rapid flight. There, deep in thought, they sat
with eyes sad fixed on the lessening shores, and ru-
minated even to melancholy. The dismal war returns
upon their thoughts, with the pleasant days of '76,
then bright with hope, but, now, alas! all darkened
in despair. "'Twas then," said they, "we first
approached these coasts, shaded far and wide with
our navies, nodding tall and stately over the heaving
surge. From their crowded decks looked forth
myriads of blooming warriors, eagerly gazing on the
lovely shores, the farms, and flocks, and domes, fondly
regarded as their own, with all the beauteous maids,
the easy purchase of a bloodless strife! But ah, vain
hope! Washington met us in his strength. His people poured around him as the brindled sons of the
desert around their sire when he lifts his terrible
voice, and calls them from their dens, to aid him in
war against the mighty rhinoceros. The battle raged

along a thousand fields—a thousand streams ran purple with British gore. And now of all our blooming warriors, alas! how few remain! Pierced by the fatal rifle, far the greater part now press their bloody beds. There, each on his couch of honour, lie those who were once the flower of our host. There lies the gallant Frazer, the dauntless Ferguson, the accomplished Donop, and that pride of youth, the generous Andre, with thousands equally brave and good. But, O! ye dear partners of this cruel strife, though fallen, ye are not forgotten! Often, with tears do we see you still, as when you rejoiced with us at the feast, or fought by our sides in battle. But vain was all our valour. God fought for Washington. Hence our choicest troops are fallen before him; and we, the sad remains of war, are now returning, inglorious, to our native shores. Land of the graves of Heroes, farewell! Ghosts of the noble dead! chide not the steps of our departure! ye are left: but it is in the land of brothers, who often mourned the death which their valour gave. But now the unnatural strife is past, and peace returns. And O! with peace may that spirit return which once warmed the hearts of Americans towards their British brethren, when the sight of our tall ships was wont to spread joy along their shores; and when the planter, viewing his cotton-covered fields, rejoiced that he was preparing employment and bread for thousands of the poor!!"

The hostile fleets and armies thus withdrawn, and the Independence of his country acknowledged; Washington proceeded, at the command of Congress, to disband the army! To this event, though of all others the dearest to his heart, he had ever looked forward with trembling anxiety. Loving his soldiers as his children, how could he tell them the painful truth which the poverty of his country had imposed on him? How could he tell them, that after all they had done and suffered with him, they must now ground their arms, and return home, many of them without a decent suit on their backs, or a penny in their pockets?

But he was saved the pain of making this communication; for they soon received it from another quarter, and with circumstances calculated to kindle the fiercest indignation against their country. Letters were industriously circulated through the army, painting in the strongest colours, their unparalleled sufferings, and the ingratitude of Congress.

"Confiding in her honour," said the writer, did you not cheerfully enlist in the service of your country, and for her dear sake encounter all the evils of a soldier's life? Have you not beaten the ice-bound road full many a wintry day, without a shoe to your bleeding feet; and wasted the long bitter night, without a tent, to shelter your heads from the pelting storm? Have you not borne the brunt of many a bloody fight, and, from the hands of hard struggling foes, torn the glorious prize, your country's independence? And now after all—after wasting in her service the flower of your days—with bodies broken under arms, and bones with the pains and aches of a seven year's war, will you suffer yourselves to be sent home in rags to your families, to spend the sad remains of life in poverty and scorn?—No! my brothers in arms! I trust you will not. I trust you bear no such coward minds. I trust, that after having fought so bravely for the rights of others, you will now fight as bravely for your own rights. And now is the accepted time and golden hour of redress, while you have weapons in your hands, the strength of an army to support you, and a beloved general at your head, ready to lead you to that justice which you owe to yourselves, and, which you have so long but vainly expected from an ungrateful country."

These letters produced, as might have been expected, a most alarming effect. Rage, like a fire in secret, began to burn throughout the camp. Washington soon perceived it. He discovered it in his

Soldiers, as, gathered into groupes, they stood and murmured over their grievances, while, with furious looks and gestures, they stamped on the earth, and hurled their curses against Congress. Gladdening at such success of his first letters, the writer instantly sent around a second series, still more artful and inflammatory than the first. The passions of the army now rose to a height that threatened instantaneous explosion. But still their eyes, beaming reverence and love, were turned towards their honoured chief, to whom they had ever looked as to a father.

Often had they marked his tears, as, visiting their encampments, he beheld them suffering and sinking under fevers and fluxes, for want of clothes and provisions. Often, had they hushed their complaints, trusting to his promises that Congress would still remember them. But behold! his promises and their hopes are all alike abortive!

And will not Washington, the friend of justice and father of his army, avenge them on a government which has thus basely defrauded them, and deceived him? There needed but a glance of his approbation to set the whole army in motion. Instantly with fixed bayonets they would have hurled the hated Congress from their seats, and placed their beloved Washington on the throne of St. Tammany. Here, no doubt, the tempter flashed the dangerous diadem before the eyes of our countryman. But religion at the same time, pointed him to the great lover of order, holding up that crown, in comparison of which the diadems of kings are but dross. Animated with such hopes he had long cherished that ardent philanthropy which sighs for liberty to all countries, and especially to his own. For Liberty he had fought and conquered; and now considered it, with all its blessings, as at hand. "Yet a little while, and America shall become the glory of the earth—a nation of Brothers, enjoying the golden reign of equal laws, and rejoicing under their own vine and fig-tree, and no tyrant to

12

make them afraid. And shall these glorious prospects be darkened? shall they be darkened by Washington! shall he, ever the friend of his country, become her bitterest enemy, by fixing upon her again the iron yoke of monarchy? shall he! the father of his army, become their assassin, by establishing a government that shall swallow up their liberties for ever?"

The idea filled his soul with horror. Instead, therefore, of tamely yielding to the wishes of his army to their own ruin, he bravely opposes them to their true good : and instead of drinking in, with traitorous smile, the hozannas that would' have made him king, he darkens his brow of parental displeasure at their impiety. He flies to extinguish their rising rebellion. He addresses letters to the officers of the army, desiring them to meet him at an appointed time and place. Happily for America, the voice of Washington still sounded in their ears, as the voice of a father. His officers, to a man, all gathered around him; while, with a countenance inspiring veneration and love, he arose and addressed the eager listening chiefs. He began with reminding them of the great object for which they had first drawn their swords, i. e. the liberty of their country. He applauded that noble spirit with which they had submitted to so many privations—combated so many dangers—and overcome so many difficulties. And now, said he, after having thus waded, like Israel of old, through a red sea of blood, and withstood the thundering Sinais of British fury; after having crushed the fiery serpents of Indian rifles, and trampled down those insidious Amalekites, the tories—after having travelled through a howling wilderness of war, and, with the ark of your country's liberties in camp, safely arrived on the borders of Canaan, and in sight of the glorious end of all your labours, will you now give yourselves up the dupes of a "British emissary," and for the sordid flesh-pots of a few months' pay, rush into civil war, and fall back to a worse than Egyptian bondage? No! my brave countrymen: I trust you will not: I trust, that an army so famed throughout the world for patriotism, will yet maintain its reputation. I trust, that your behaviour on this last, this most trying occasion, will fill up the measure of your heroism, and stamp the American character with never dying fame. You have achieved miracles. But a greater miracle still remains to be achieved. We have had the glory to conquer our enemies; now for the greater glory to conquer ourselves. Other armies, after subduing the enemies of their country, have themselves, for power and plunder, become her tyrants, and trampled her liberties under foot. Be it our nobler ambition, after sufferings unparalleled for our needy country, to return cheerful, though pennyless, to our homes; and patiently wait the rewards which her gratitude will, one day, assuredly bestow. In the mean time, beating our swords into ploughshares, and our bayonets into reaping hooks, let us, as peaceful citizens, cultivate those fields from which, as victorious soldiers, we lately drove the enemy. Thence, as from the noblest of theatres, you will display a spectacle of patriotism never seen before. You will teach the delighted world, that men are capable of finding a heaven in noble actions: and you will give occasion to posterity to say; when speaking of your present behaviour, had this day been wanting, the triumph of our fathers' virtues would have been incomplete."

As he spoke, his cheeks, naturally pale, were reddened over with virtue's pure vermillion: while his eyes, of cerulean blue, were kindled up with those indescribable fires which fancy lends to an angel orator, animating poor mortals, to the sublimest of god-like deeds. His words, were not in vain. From lips of wisdom, and long-tried love, like his, such counsel wrought as though an oracle had spoken. Instantly a committee of the whole was formed, with general Knox at their head, who, in thirty minutes, reported the following resolutions, which were unanimously adopted:

"Resolved—that having engaged in the war from motives of the purest love and zeal for the rights of man, no circumstance of distress or danger shall ever induce us to sully the glory we have acquired at the price of our blood, and eight years' faithful service.

"Resolved—that we continue to have an unshaken confidence in the justice of congress and our country.

"Resolved—that we view with abhorrence, and reject with disdain, the infamous proposition contained in a late anonymous address to the officers of the army."

The officers then hasted back to their troops, who had been impatiently expecting them; and related Washington's speech. They also stated as his firm conviction, that " the claims of every soldier would be liquidated; his accounts accurately ascertained; and adequate funds provided for the payment of them, as soon as the circumstances of the nation would permit.

The soldiers listened to this communication with attention: and heard the close of it without a murmur. "They had no great opinion, they said, of congress—but having gone such lengths for duty and old George. they supposed they might as well now go a little farther, and make thorough work of it. A little pay would, to be sure, have been very welcome: and it was a poor military chest that could not afford a single dollar, especially as some of them had hundreds of miles to travel to reach their homes. But surely the people won't let us starve for a meal's victuals by the way, especially after we have been so long fighting their battles. So, in God's name, we'll even shoulder our knapsacks, whenever our general shall say the word."

The next day, the breaking up of the army began, which was conducted in the following manner: The troops after breakfast were ordered under arms. On receiving notice that they were ready to move, Washington with his aids, rode out on the plains of their encampment, where he sat on his horse awaiting their arrival. The troops got in motion, and with fifes and muffled drums playing the mournful air of Roslin Castle, marched up for the last time, into his presence. Every countenance was shrouded in sorrow. At a signal given, they grounded their arms. Then, waving their hats, and faintly crying out "God save great Washington," through watery eyes they gave him a long adieu, and wheeled off in files for their native homes. With pensive looks his eye pursued them as they retired, wide spreading over the fields. But when he saw those brave troops who had so long obeyed him, and who had just given such an evidence of their affection—when he saw them slowly descending behind the distant hills, shortly to disappear for ever, then nature stirred all the father within him, and gave him up to tears. But he wept not "as those without hope." He rejoiced in the remembrance of HIM who treasures up the toils of the virtuous, and will, one day, bestow that reward which, "this world cannot give."

But the whole army was not disbanded at once. Shortly after this he went down to New York, to finish what remained of his duty as commander in chief, and to prepare to return home. On the last day that he was there, it being known that he meant to set out for Virginia at one o'clock, all his officers, who happened to be in town, assembled at Francis's tavern, where he lodged, to bid him a last farewell. About half after twelve o'clock the general entered the room, where an elegant collation was spread: but none tasted it. Conversation was attempted: but it failed. As the clock struck one, the general went to the side-board, and filling out some wine, turned to his officers, and begged they would join him in a glass. Then, with a look of sorrow and a faltering voice, he said, " Well my brave brothers in arms, we part——perhaps to meet in this life no more. And now I pray God to take you all in his holy keeping, and render your latter days as prosperous as the past have been glorious."

Soon as they had drunk, he beckoned to general Knox, who approached and pressed his hand in tears of delicious silence. The officers all followed his example; while their manly cheeks, swollen with grief, bespoke sensations too strong for utterance. This tender scene being over, he moved towards the door, followed by his officers. By this time the street from the hotel to the river was filled with light infantry, and thousands of citizens, who all attended him in silence to the water-side, where he was to take boat. Here another pleasing proof of esteem was given him. Instead of the common ferry boat, a barge magnificently decorated, was ready to receive him, with the American jack and colors flying, and manned with thirteen sea captains, all in elegant blue uniforms. On stepping aboard the barge, he turned towards the people, who stood in vast crowds on the shore : and waving his hat, bade them a silent adieu, which they in like solemn manner returned, all waving their hats, and without speaking a word. Having received their honoured freight, the sons of Neptune, ready with well poised oars, leap forward to the coxswain's call ; then, all at once falling back, with sudden stroke they flash their bending blades into the yielding flood. Swift at their stroke the barge sprung from the shore ; and, under the music of echoing row-locks, flew through the waves, followed by the eager gaze of the pensive thousands. The sighing multitude then turned away from the shore with feelings whose source they did not, perhaps, understand. But some, on returning to their homes, spoke to their listening children of what they had seen, and of the honours which belong to such virtue as Washington's.

He lodged that night at Elizabethtown, fifteen miles from New York. The next morning, elate with thoughts of home, he ascended his chariot; and with bounding steeds drove on his way through the lovely country of New Jersey. This no doubt, was the pleasantest ride by far that he had known since the dark days of '75. For though joyless winter was spread abroad, with her cold clouds, and winds shrill whistling over the flowerless fields; yet to his patriot eye the face of nature shone brighter than in latter years, when clad in springtide green and gold—for it was covered over with the bright mantle of peace. His shoulders were freed from the burden of public cares, and his heart from the anxieties of supreme command. With a father's joy he could look around on the thick settled country, with all its little ones, and flocks, and herds, now no longer exposed to danger.

"Happy farmers! the long winter of war is past and gone—the spring time of peace is returned, and the voice of her dove is heard in our land. Restore your wasted farms. Spread abroad the fertilizing manure: and prepare again to crown your war worn fields with joyful crops."

"Happy children! now pour forth again in safety to your schools. Treasure up the golden knowledge; and make yourselves the future glory and guardians of your country."

Happy citizens! hasten to rebuild the ruined temples of your God. And lift your glad songs to Him, the great ruler of war, who aided your feeble arms, and trampled down the mighty enemy beneath your feet."

But often, amidst these happy thoughts, the swift-wheeled chariot would bring him in view of fields on which his bleeding memory could not dwell without a tear. "There the battling armies met in thunder

The stormy strife was short. But yonder mournful hillocks point the place where many of our brave heroes sleep ; perhaps some good angel has whispered that their fall was not in vain."

On his journey homewards, he stopped for a moment at Philadelphia, to do an act, which to a mind proudly honest like his, must have been a sublime treat. He stopped to present to the comptroller-general an account of all the public moneys which he had spent. Though this account was in his own hand writing, and accompanied with the proper vouchers, yet it will hardly be credited by European statesmen and generals, that, in the course of an eight years war, he had spent only 12,497*l.* 8*s.* 9*d.* sterling ! !

From Philadelphia he hastened on to Annapolis, where Congress was then in session, that he might return to that honourable body the commission with which they had entrusted him.

Having always disliked parade, he wished to make his resignation in writing. But Congress, it seems, willed otherwise. To see a man voluntarily giving up power, was a spectacle not to be met with every day. And that they might have the pleasure of seeing him in this last, and perhaps greatest, act of his public life, they expressed a wish to receive his resignation from his own hand at a full audience. The next day, the 23d of December, 1783, was appointed for the purpose. At an early hour the house was crowded. The members of Congress, with the grandees of the land, filled the floors. The ladies sparkled in the galleries. At eleven o'clock, Washington was ushered into the house, and conducted to a seat which had been prepared for him, covered with red velvet. After a becoming pause, and information given by the president, that the United States in Congress assembled were ready to receive his communication, he arose; and with great brevity and modesty observed, that he had presented hi,   f before them, to resign into their hands with satisfaction the commission which, eight years before, he had accepted with diffidence. He begged to offer them his sincerest congratulations for the glorious result of their united struggles; took no part of the praise to himself; but ascribed all to the blessing of Heaven on the exertions of the nation.   Then fervently commending his dearest country to the protection of Almighty God, he bade them an affectionate farewell; and taking leave of all the employments of public life, surrendered up his commission!

Seldom has there been exhibited so charming a display of the power which pre-eminent virtue possesses over the human heart, as on this occasion. Short and simple as was the speech of Washington, yet it seems to have carried back every trembling imagination to the fearful days of '75, when the British fleets and armies were thundering on our coasts, and when nothing was talked of but slavery, confiscation, and executions. And now they saw before them the man to whom they all looked for safety in that gloomy time—who had completely answered their fond hopes—who had stood by them incorruptible and unshaken—had anticipated their mighty enemy in all his plans—had met him at every point—had thwarted, defeated, and blasted all his hopes—and, victory after victory won, had at length laid his strong legions in dust or in chains—and had secured to his country a glorious independence, with the fairest chance of being one of the most respectable and happy nations of the earth—and, in consequence of all this, had so completely won the hearts of his army and his nation, that he could perhaps have made himself their master. At all events, a Cæsar or a Cromwell would, at the hazard of a million of lives, made the sacrilegious attempt. Yet they now saw this man scorning to abuse his power to the degradation of his country,—but on the con-

trary, treating her with the most sacred respect—
dutifully bowing before her delegated presence, the
congress—cheerfully returning the commission she
had entrusted him with—piously laying down his
extensive powers at her feet—and modestly falling
back into the humble condition of the rest of her
children. The sight of their great countryman,
already so beloved, and now acting so generous, so
godlike a part, produced an effect beyond the power
of words to express. Their feelings of admiration
and affection were too delicious, too big for utterance.
Every countenaace was swollen with sentiment; and
delicious tears moistened every eye, which, though a
silent, was perhaps the richest offering of veneration
and esteem ever paid to a human being.

Having discharged this last great debt to his
country, the next morning early he ascended his
chariot; and listened with joy to the rattling wheels,
now running off his last day's journey to Mount
Vernon. Ah! could gloomy tyrants but feel what
Washington felt that day, when, sweeping along the
road, with grateful heart, he revolved the mighty
work which he had finished—his country saved and
his conscience clear; they would tear off the accursed
purple, and starting from their blood-stained thrones,
like Washington, seek true happiness in making
others happy.

O Washington! thrice glorious name,
What due rewards can man decree?
Empires are far below thy aim,
And sceptres have no charms for thee;
Duty alone has thy regard,
In her thou seek'st thy great reward.

CHAPTER XI.

Washington again on his farm—sketch of his conduct there—suggests the importance of inland navigation—companies forming—urges a reform of the old constitution—appointed President of the United States—great difficulties to encounter—gloriously surmounts them.

To be happy in every situation is a proof of wisdom seldom afforded by man. It proves that the heart is set on that which alone can ever completely satisfy it, i. e. the imitation of God in benevolent and useful life. This was the happy case with Washington. To establish in his country the golden reign of liberty is his grand wish. In the accomplishment of this he seeks his happiness. He abhors war; but, if war be necessary, to this end he bravely encounters it. His ruling passion must be obeyed. He beat his ploughshare into a sword, and exchanged the peace and pleasures of his farm for the din and dangers of the camp. Having won the great prize for which he contended, he returns to his plough. His military habits are laid by with the same ease as he would throw off an old coat. The camp with all its parade and noise, is forgotten. He awakes, in his silent chambers at Mount Vernon, without sighing for the sprightly drums and fifes that used to salute him every morning. Happy among his domestics, he does not regret the shining ranks of patriot soldiers that used to pay him homage. The useful citizen is the high character he wishes to act—his sword turned into a ploughshare is his favourite instrument; and his beloved farm his stage. Agriculture had been always his delight. To breathe the pure healthful air of a farm, perfumed with odorous flowers, and enriched with golden harvests, and with numerous flocks and herds, appeared to him a life nearest connected with individual and national happiness. To this great object he turns all his attention—bends all his exertions. He writes to the most skilful farmers,

not only in America, but in England (for Washington
was incapable of bearing malice against a people who
had been reconciled to his country;) he writes, I say,
to the ablest farmers in America and England, for
instructions how best to cultivate and improve his
lands—what grains, what grasses, what manures
would best suit his soils; what shrubs are fittest for
fences, and what animals for labour.

But, to a soul large and benevolent like his, to
beautify his own farm, and to enrich his own family,
seemed like doing nothing. To see the whole nation
engaged in glorious toils, filling themselves with
plenty, and inundating the sea ports with food and
raiment for the poor and needy of distant nations—
this was his godlike ambition. But, knowing that his
beloved countrymen could not long enjoy the honour
and advantage of such glorious toils, unless they could
easily convey their swelling harvests to their own
markets, he hastened to rouse them to a proper sense
of the infinite importance of forming canals and cuts
between all the fine rivers that run throught he United States.   To give the greater weight to his counsel, he had first ascended the sources of those great
rivers—ascertained the distance between them—the
obstacles in the way of navigation—and the probable
expense of removing them.

Agreeably to his wishes, two wealthy companies
were soon formed to extend the navigation of James
River and Potomac, the noblest rivers in Virginia.
Struck with the exceeding benefit which both themselves and their country would speedily derive from
a plan which he had not only suggested, but had
taken such pains and expense to recommend, they
pressed him to accept one hundred and fifty shares
of the company's stock, amounting to near 40,000
dollars! But he instantly refused it, saying, "what
will the world think if they should hear that I have
taken 40,000 dollars for this affair? Will they not be
apt to suspect, on my next proposition, that money

is my motive? Thus, for the sake of money, which
indeed I never coveted from my country, I may lose
the power to do her some service, which may be
worth more than all money!!"

But, while engaged in this goodly work, he was
suddenly alarmed by the appearance of an evil, which
threatened to put an end to all his well-meant labours
for ever—this was, the incipient dissolution of the
federal government!! The framers of that fair but
flimsy fabric, having put it together according to the
square and compass of equal rights, and mutual
interests, thought they had done enough. The good
sense and virtue of the nation, it was supposed, would
form a foundation of rock whereon it would safely
rest, in spite of all commotions, foreign or domestic.

"But, alas!" said Washington, "experience has
shown, that men unless constrained, will seldom do
what is for their own good. With joy I once beheld
my country feeling the liveliest sense of her rights,
and maintaining them with a spirit apportioned to.
their worth. With joy I have seen all the wise men
of Europe looking on her with admiration, and all the
good with hope, that her fair example would rege-
nerate the whole world, and restore the blessings of
equal government to long oppressed humanity. But
alas! in place of maintaining this glorious attitude,
America is herself rushing into disorder and dissolution. We have powers sufficient for self-defence and
glory; but those powers are not exerted. For fear
congress should abuse it, the people will not trust
their power with congress. Foreigners insult and
injure us with impunity; for congress has no power
to chastise them.—Ambitious men stir up factions.
Congress possesses no power to coerce them. Public
creditors call for their money. Congress has no
power to collect it. In short, we cannot long subsist.
as a nation, without lodging somewhere a power
that may command the full energies of the nation for
defence from all its enemies, and for the supply of all

its wants. The people will soon be tired of such a government. They will sigh for a change : and many of them already begin to talk of monarchy, without horror !"

In this, as in all cases of apprehended danger, his pen knew no rest. The leading characters of the nation were roused : and a CONVENTION was formed, of deputies from the several states, to revise and amend the general government. Of this convention Washington was unanimously chosen president.— Their session commenced in Philadelphia, May, 1787, and ended in October. The fruit of their six months labour was the present excellent CONSTITUTION, which was no sooner adopted, than the eyes of the whole nation were fixed on him for president.

Being now in his 57th year, and wedded to his farm and family, he had no wish to enter again into the cares and dangers of public life. Ease was now become almost as necessary as it was dear to him. His reputation was already at the highest; and as to money, in the service of his country he had always refused it. These things considered, together with his acknowledged modesty and disinterestedness, we can hardly doubt the correctness of his declaration, that, " the call to the magistracy was the most unwelcome he had ever heard."

However, as soon as it was officially notified to him, in the spring of 1789, that he was unanimously elected President of the United States, and that Congress, then sitting in New York, was impatient to see him in the chair, he set out for that city. Then all along the roads where he passed, were seen the most charming proofs of that enthusiasm with which the hearts of all delighted to honour him. If it was only said, "General Washington is coming," it was enough. The inhabitants all hastened from their houses to the highways, to have a sight of their great countryman; while the people of the towns, hearing of his approach, sallied out, horse and foot, to meet him. In eager throngs, men, women and children, pressed upon his steps, as waves in crowding ridges pursue the course of a ship through the ocean. And as a new succession of waves is ever ready to take the place of those which have just ended their chase in playful foam, so it was with the ever-gathering crowds that followed their Washington.

"On reaching the western banks of the Schuylkill," said a gentleman who was present, "I was astonished at the concourse of people that overspread the country, apparently from Gray's ferry to the city. Indeed one would have thought that the whole population of Philadelphia was come out to meet him. And to see so many thousands of people on foot, on horseback, and in coaches, all voluntarily waiting upon and moving along with one man, struck me with strangely agreeable sensations. Surely, thought I, there must be a divinity in goodness, that mankind should thus delight to honour it."

His reception at Trenton was more than flattering. It was planned, they said, by the ladies, and indeed bore marks that it could have been done only by them. The reader must remember, that it was near this place that the fair sex in '76 suffered such cruel indignities from the enemy; and that it was here that Providence in the same year enabled Washington so severely to chastise them for it. The women are not apt to forget their benefactors. Hearing that Washington was on his way to Trenton, they instantly held a caucus among themselves, to devise ways and means to display their gratitude to him. Under their direction, the bridge over the Sanpink, (a narrow creek running through Trenton, upon whose opposite banks Washington and the British once fought,) was decorated with a triumphal arch, with this inscription in large figures:

DECEMBER 26, 1776.

THE HERO WHO DEFENDED THE MOTHERS,
WILL ALSO PROTECT THE DAUGHTERS.

He approached the bridge on its south side, amidst the heartiest shouts of congratulating thousands; while on the north side were drawn up several hundreds of little girls, dressed in snow-white robes, with temples adorned with garlands, and baskets of flowers on their arms. Just behind them stood long rows of young virgins, whose fair faces, of sweetest red and white, highly animated by the occasion, looked quite angelic—and, behind them in crowds, stood their venerable mothers. As Washington slowly drove off the bridge, the female voices all began, sweet as the first wakings of the Eolian harp: and thus they rolled the song:

" Welcome, mighty chief! once more
Welcome to this grateful shore.
Now no mercenary foe
Aims again the fatal blow,
Aims at thee the fatal blow.

Virgins fair, and matrons grave,
(These thy conquering arm did save!)
Build for thee triumphal bowers,
Strew, ye fair, his way with flowers;
Strew your hero's way with flowers.

While singing the last lines, they strewed the way with flowers before him.

Some have said that they could see in his altered looks, that he remembered the far different scenes of '76; for that they saw him wipe a tear. No doubt it was the sweet tear of gratitude to him who had preserved him to see this happy day.

At New York the behaviour of the citizens was equally expressive of the general veneration and esteem. The ships in the harbour were all dressed in their flags and streamers; and the wharves where he landed were richly decorated. At the water's edge he was received by an immense concourse of the joyful citizens; and, amidst the mingled thunder of guns and acclamations, was conducted to his lodgings. Such honours, would have intoxicated most men : but to a mind like his, habitually conversant with the far sublimer subjects of the Christian philosophy, they must have looked quite puerile.   Indeed it appears from a note made in his journal that very evening, that he regarded all these marks of public favour rather as calls to humility than pride.   " The display of boats on this occasion," says he, " with vocal and instrumental music on board, the decorations of the ships, the roar of cannon, and the loud acclamations of the people, as I passed along the wharves, gave me as much pain as pleasure, contemplating the probable reverse of this scene after all my endeavour to do good."

It was on the 23d of April, 1789, that he arrived in New York : and on the 30th, after taking the oath, as president of the United States, to preserve, protect, and defend the constitution, he entered upon the duties of his office.

As things then stood, even his bitterest enemies, if he had any, might have said, " happy man be his dole !" for he came to the helm in a perilous and fearful season.   Like chaos, " in the olden time," our government was " without form and void : and darkness dwelt upon the face of the deep."   Enemies innumerable threatened the country, both from within, and without, abroad and at home—the people of three continents at daggers drawn with the young republic of America !

The pirates of Morocco laying their uncircumcised hands on our rich commerce in the Mediterranean.

The British grumbling and threatening war.

The Spaniards shutting up the Mississippi !

The Kentuckians in great warmth, threatening to break the Union, and join the Spaniards !

The Indian nations, from Canada to Georgia, unburying the tomahawk !

North Carolina and Rhode Island, blowing on the confederacy ! strong parties in other states against it !

13*

—and an alarming insurrection in Massachusetts!—
While, to combat all these enemies, the United States
had but 600 regular troops!! and, though eighty
millions of dollars in debt, they had not one cent in
the treasury!!! Here certainly, if ever, was the time
to try a man's soul. But Washington despaired not.
Glowing with the love of his country, and persuaded
that his country still enjoyed an opportunity to be
great and happy, he resolved, whatever it might cost
him, that nothing should be wanting on his part to
fill up the measure of her glory. But first of all, in
his inaugural speech, he called upon Congress and
his countrymen, to look up to God for his blessing;
next, as to themselves, to be most industrious, honourable, and united, as became men responsible to
ages yet unborn, for all the blessings of a republican
government, now, and perhaps for the last time, at
stake, on their wisdom and virtue;—then as to himself; "I feel," said he, " my incompetency of political
skill and abilities. Integrity and firmness are all I
can promise. These, I know, will never forsake me,
although I may be deserted by all men: and of the
consolations to be derived from these, under no circumstances can the world ever deprive me."—And
last of all, as, in a crazy ship at sea, tossed by furious
winds, no pilot can save without the aid of able sea
men, Washington prudently rallied around him the
wisest of all his countrymen.

Mr. Jefferson, Secretary of Foreign Affairs.
Col. Hamilton, Secretary of the Treasury.
Gen. Knox, Secretary of War.
Edmund Randolph, Attorney General.
John Jay, Chief Justice.
John Rutledge,
James Wilson,
John Cushing, } Associate Judges.
Robert Harrison,
John Blair,
These judicious preparations being made for the

storm, (Heaven's blessing invoked, and the ablest
pilots embarked with him,) Washington then seized
the helm, with a gallant hard-a-lee; luffed up his
ship at once to the gale, hoping yet to shoot the
hideous gulfs that threatened all around.

His first attention was turned to the call of
Humanity, i. e. to satisfy and make peace with the
Indians.   This was soon done; partly by presents,
and by establishing, in their country, houses of fair
trade, which, by preventing frauds, prevent those
grudges that lead to private murders, and thence to
public disturbances and wars.   Some of the Indian
tribes, despising these friendly efforts of Washington,
were obliged to be drubbed into peace, which service
was done for them by General Wayne, in 1794—
but not until many lives had been lost in preceding
defeats; owing chiefly, it was said, to the very
intemperate passions and potations of some of their
officers.   However, after the first shock, the loss of
these poor souls was not much lamented.   Tall young
fellows, who could easily get their half dollar a day
at the healthful and glorious labours of the plough,
to go and enlist and rust among the lice and itch of
a camp, for four dollars a month, were certainly not
worth their country's crying about.

Washington's friendly overtures to Spain were
equally fortunate.   Believing that he desired nothing
but what was perfectly just, and what both God and
man would support him in, she presently agreed to
negociate.   The navigation of the Mississippi was
given up.   The Kentuckians were satisfied: and
Spain and the United States lived on good terms all
the rest of his days.

Washington then tried his hands with the British.
But alas! he soon found that they were not made of
such pliable stuff as the Indians and Spaniards.   Nor
had he the British alone to complain of.   He presently found it as hard to satisfy his own countrymen, in
the matter of a treaty, as to please them.

For whether it was that the two nations still retained a most unchristian recollection of what they had suffered from one another during the past war— or whether, more unchristianly still, they felt the odious spirit of rivals, and sickened at each other's prosperity—or whether each nation thought that the ships of the other were navigated by their seamen; but so it was, that the prejudices of the two people, though sprung from the same progenitors, ran so high as to render it extremely difficult for Washington to settle matters between them. But it was at length happily effected, without the horrors of another war. Though the treaty which brought about this desirable event was entirely execrated by great numbers of sensible and honest men no doubt, yet Washington, led, as he says, by duty and humanity, ratified it.

If the signing of the treaty displayed his firmness, the operation of it has, perhaps, shown his wisdom. For, surely, since that time, no country like this ever so progressed in the public and private blessings of industry, wealth, population, and morals. Whether greater, or, indeed, equal blessings would have resulted from a bloody war with England at that time, let others determine.

But scarcely had Washington got clear of his embarrassments with Britain, before still worse were thrown in his way by France.

The cause was this. "The French army," as Doctor Franklin observes, "having served an apprenticeship to Liberty, in America, on going back to France, set up for themselves." Throughout the kingdom, wherever they went, they could talk of nothing but the Americans. "Ah, happy people!" said they, "neither oppressing nor oppressed, they mingle together as one great family of brothers. Every man is free. Every man labours for himself, and wipes with joy the sweat from his brow, because 'tis the earnest of plenteous food and clothing, education, and delights, for his children!"

The people every where listened with eagerness to these descriptions of American happiness, and sighed to think of their own wretchedness. The smothered fire soon broke out. The press teemed with papers and pamphlets on the rights of Man— the true ends of government,—and the blessings of Liberty. The eyes of the great nation were presently opened to a sight of her degraded and wretched state. Then suddenly springing up, like a mighty giantess from the hated bed of violation and dishonour, she began a course of vengeance as terrible as it had been long delayed. The unfortunate king and queen were quickly brought low. The heads of her tyrants every where bounded on the floors of the guillotine; while in every place dogs licked the blood of nobles: and the bodies of great lords were scattered like dung over the face of the earth.

Fearing that if France were suffered to go on at this rate, there would not in a little time, be a crown left in Europe, the crowned heads all confederated to arrest her progress. The whole surrounding world, both by land and water, was in commotion: and tremendous fleets and armies poured in from every side, to overwhelm her. With unanimity and valour equal to their dangers, the war-loving Gauls rushed forth in crowding millions to meet their foes. The mighty armies joined in battle, appearing to the terrified eye, as if the whole human race were rushing together for mutual destruction. But not content with setting the eastern world on fire, the furious combatants (like Milton's warring Spirits tearing up and flinging mountains and islands at each other) flew to America to seize and drag her into their war.

Flaming on this errand, Mr. Genet lighted on our continent as an envoy from France. He was received with joy as a brother republican. The people every where welcomed him as the representative of a beloved nation, to whom, under God, they owed their liberties. Grand dinners were given—sparkling bumpers were filled—and standing up round the vast convivial board, with joined hands, and cheeks glowing with friendship and the generous juice, they rent the air with—"health and fraternity to the sister republics of France and America."

Washington joined in the general hospitality to the stranger. He extolled the valour, and congratulated the victories of his brave countrymen. "Born, sir," said he, "in a land of Liberty, for whose sake I have spent the best years of my life in war, I cannot but feel a trembling anxiety whenever I see an oppressed people drawing their swords and rearing aloft the sacred banners of freedom."

Enraptured at finding in America such a cordial spirit towards his country, Mr. Genet instantly set himself to call it into the fullest exertion. And by artfully ringing the changes on British cruelty, and French generosity, to the Americans, he so far succeeded as to prevail on some persons in Charleston to commence the equipment of privateers against the British. Dazzled by the lustre of false gratitude to one nation, they lost sight of their horrid injustice to another: and during the profoundest peace between England and America, when the American planters, by their flour, rice, and cotton, were making money almost as fast as if they had mints upon their estates; and when, on the other hand, the British artisans were driving on their manufactures day and night for the Americans—in this sacred season and blissful state of things, certain persons in Charleston began to equip privateers against England.

Grieved that his countrymen should be capable of such an outrage against justice, against humanity, and every thing sacred among men; and equally grieved to see them so far forget, so far belittle themselves as to become willing cat's paws of one nation, to tear another to pieces, he instantly issued his proclamation, stating it as the "duty, and therefore the interest of the United States, to preserve the strictest neutrality between the belligerents: and prohibiting the citizens of the United States, from all manner of interference in the unhappy contest."

This so enraged Mr. Genet, that he threatened to appeal from the president to the people! i. e. in plain English, to try to overthrow the government of the United States!!

But, thank God, the American people were too wise and virtuous to hear these things without feeling and expressing a suitable indignation. They rallied around their beloved president; and soon gave this most inconsiderate stranger to understand, that he had insulted the sacred person of their father.

Washington bore this insult with his usual good temper! but at the same time took such prudent measures with the French government, that Mr. Genet was quickly recalled.

Having at length attained the acme of all his wishes—having lived to see a general and efficient government adopted, and for eight years in successful operation, exalting his country from the brink of infamy and ruin to the highest ground of prosperity and honour, both at home and abroad—abroad, peace with Britain—with Spain—and, some slight heart burnings excepted, peace with France, and with all the world: at home, peace with the Indians—our shining ploughshares laying open the best treasures of the earth—our ships flying over every sea—distant nations feeding on our bread, and manufacturing our staples—our revenue rapidly increasing with our credit, religion, learning, arts, and whatever tends to national glory and happiness, he determined to lay down that load of public care which he had borne so long, and which, now in his 66th year, he found was growing too heavy for him. But feeling towards his countrymen the solicitude of a father for his children, over whom he had long watched, but whom he was about to leave to themselves; and fearing, on the one hand, that they might go astray, and hoping, on the other, that from his long labours of love, he might be permitted to impart the counsels of his long experience, he drew up for them a farewell address, which the filial piety of the nation has since called " his Legacy."

As this little piece, about the length of an ordinary sermon, may do as much good to the people of America as any sermon ever preached, that Divine one on the mount excepted, I shall offer no apology for laying it before them; especially as I well know that they will all read it with the feelings of children reading the last letter of a once loved father now in his grave. And who knows but it may check for a while the fatal flame of discord which has destroyed all the once glorious republics of antiquity, and here now at length in the United States has caught upon the last republic that is left on the face of the earth.

WASHINGTON'S LAST WORDS

TO THE PEOPLE OF THE UNITED STATES.

September, 1796.

"Friends and Fellow Citizens,

" The period for a new election of a citizen, to administer the executive government of the United States, being not far distant—and the time actually arrived when your thoughts must be employed in designating the person who is to be clothed with that important trust—it appears to me proper, especially as it may conduce to a more distinct expression of the public voice, that I should now apprise you of the resolution I have formed, to decline being considered among the number of those out of whom a choice is to be made.

" I beg you, at the same time, to do me the justice to be assured, that this resolution has not been taken without a strict regard to all the considerations appertaining to the relation which binds a dutiful citizen to his country; and that, in withdrawing the tender of service, which silence in my situation might imply, I am influenced by no diminution of zeal for your future interest, no deficiency of grateful respect for your past kindness; but am supported by a full conviction, that the step is compatible with both.

" The acceptance of, and continuance hitherto in, the office to which your suffrages have twice called me, have been a uniform sacrifice of inclination to the opinion of duty, and to a deference for what appeared to be your desire. I constantly hoped, that it would have been much earlier in my power, consistently with motives which I was not at liberty

14

to disregard, to return to that retirement from which I had been reluctantly drawn. The strength of my inclination to do this previous to the last election, had even led to the preparation of an address to declare it to you. But mature reflection on the then perplexed and critical posture of our affairs with foreign nations, and the unanimous advice of persons entitled to my confidence, impelled me to abandon the idea.

" I rejoice that the state of your concerns, external as well as internal, no longer renders the pursuit of inclination incompatible with the sentiment of duty or propriety; and am persuaded, whatever partiality may be retained for my services, that, in the present circumstances of our country, you will not disapprove my determination to retire.

" The impressions with which I first undertook the arduous trust, were explained on the proper occasions. In the discharge of this trust, I will only say, that I have, with good intentions, contributed towards the organization and administration' of the government, the best exertions of which a very fallible judgment was capable. Not unconscious, in the outset, of the inferiority of my qualifications, experience in my own eyes, perhaps still more in the eyes of others, has strengthened the motives to diffidence of myself: and every day the increasing weight of years admonishes me more and more that the shade of retirement is as necessary to me as it will be welcome. Satisfied that if any circumstances have given peculiar value to my services, they were temporary, I have the consolation to believe, that while choice and prudence invite me to quit the political scene, patriotism does not forbid it.

" In looking forward to the moment which is intended to terminate the career of my public life, my feelings do not permit me to suspend the deep acknowledgment of that debt of gratitude which I owe to my beloved country, for the many honours it has conferred upon me; still more for the steadfast confidence with which it has supported me; and for the opportunities I have thence enjoyed of manifesting my inviolable attachment, by services faithful and persevering, though in usefulness unequal to my zeal. If benefits have resulted to our country from these services, let it always be remembered to your praise, and as an instructive example in our annals, that, under circumstances, in which the passions, agitated in every direction, were liable to mislead—amidst appearances sometimes dubious—vicissitudes of fortune often discouraging—in situations in which not unfrequently want of success has countenanced the spirit of criticism—the constancy of your support was the essential prop of the efforts, and a guarantee of the plans by which they were effected. Profoundly penetrated with this idea, I shall carry it with me to my grave, as a strong incitement to unceasing vows that Heaven may continue to you the choicest tokens of its beneficence; that your union and brotherly affection may be perpetual; that the free constitution, which is the work of your hands, may be sacredly maintained; that its administration, in every department, may be stamped with wisdom and virtue; that, in fine, the happiness of the people of these states, under the auspices of Heaven, may be made complete, by so careful a preservation and so prudent a use of liberty, as will acquire to them the glory of recommending it to the applause, the affection, and the adoption of every nation which is yet a stranger to it.

"Here, perhaps, I ought to stop. But a solicitude for your welfare, which cannot end but with my life, and the apprehension of danger, natural to that solicitude, urge me, on an occasion like the present, to offer to your solemn contemplation, and to recommend to your frequent review, some sentiments, which are the result of much reflection, of no inconsiderable observation, and which appear to me all important to the permanency of your felicity as a people. These will be offered to you with the more freedom, as you can only see in them the disinterested warnings of a parting friend, who can possibly have no personal motive to bias his counsel. Nor can I forget, as an encouragement to it, your indulgent reception of my sentiments on a former and not dissimilar occasion.

" Interwoven as is the love of liberty with every ligament of your hearts, no recommendation of mine is necessary to fortify or confirm the attachment.

" The unity of government, which constitutes you one people, is also now dear to you. It is justly so ; for it is a main pillar in the edifice of your real independence; the support of your tranquillity at home, your peace abroad ; of your safety ; of your prosperity ; of that very liberty which you so highly prize. But as it is easy to foresee, that from different causes, and from different quarters, much pains will be taken, many artifices employed, to weaken in your minds the conviction of this truth ; as this is the point in your political fortress, against which the batteries of internal and external enemies will be most constantly and actively (though often covertly and insidiously) directed ; it is of infinite moment, that you should properly estimate the immense value of your national union, to your collective and individual happiness ; that you should cherish a cordial, habitual, and immoveable attachment to it ; accustoming yourselves to think and speak of it as of the palladium of your political safety and prosperity ; watching for its preservation with jealous anxiety ; discountenancing whatever may suggest even a suspicion that it can in any event be abandoned ; and indignantly frowning upon the first dawning of every attempt to alien any portion of our country from the rest, or to enfeeble the sacred ties which now link together the various parts.

"For this you have every inducement of sympathy and interest. Citizens, by birth or choice, of a common country, that country has a right to concentrate your affections. The name of AMERICAN, which belongs to you in your national capacity, must always exalt the just pride of patriotism, more than any appellation derived from local discriminations. With slight shades of difference, you have the same religion, manners, habits and political principles. You have, in a common cause, fought and triumphed together. The independence and liberty you possess are the work of joint councils, and joint efforts—of common dangers, sufferings and successes.

"But these considerations, however powerfully they address themselves to your sensibility, are greatly outweighed by those which apply more immediately to your interest. Here every portion of our country finds the most commanding motives for carefully guarding and preserving the union of the whole.

"The NORTH, in an unrestrained intercourse with the SOUTH, protected by the equal laws of a common government, finds in the productions of the latter, great additional resources of maritime and commercial enterprize, and precious materials of manufacturing industry. The SOUTH, in the same intercourse benefiting by the agency of the NORTH, sees its agriculture grow, and its commerce expand. Turning partly into its own channels the seamen of the NORTH, it finds its particular navigation invigorated: and while it contributes, in different ways, to nourish and increase the general mass of the national navigation, it looks forward to the protection of a maritime strength, to which itself is unequally adapted.—The EAST, in a like intercourse with the WEST, already finds, and in the progressive improvement of interior communications, by land and water, will more and more find a valuable vent for the commodities which it brings from abroad, or manufactures at home.—

The WEST derives from the EAST supplies requisite
to its growth and comfort: and what is, perhaps, of
still greater consequence, it must of necessity owe
the SECURE enjoyment of indispensible OUTLETS for
its own productions, to the weight, influence, and
the future maritime strength of the Atlantic side of
the Union, directed by an indissoluble community of
interest, as ONE NATION. Any other tenure, by which
the WEST can hold this essential advantage, whether
derived from its own separate strength, or from an
apostate and unnatural connexion with any foreign
power must be intrinsically precarious.

  "While then every part of our country thus feels
an immediate and particular interest in union, all the
parties combined cannot fail to find, in the united
mass of means and efforts, greater strength, greater
resources, proportionably greater security from external danger, a less frequent interruption of their peace
by foreign nations. And, what is of inestimable
value, they must derive from union an exemption
from those broils and wars between themselves,
which so frequently afflict neighbouring countries,
not tied together by the same government; which
their own rivalships alone would be sufficient to produce, but which opposite foreign alliances, attachments, and intrigues, would stimulate and embitter.
Hence, likewise, they will avoid the necessity of
those overgrown military establishments, which,
under any form of government, are inauspicious to
liberty: and which are to be regarded as particularly
hostile to republican liberty. In this sense it is, that
your union ought to be considered as a main prop of
your liberty, and that the love of the one ought to
endear to you the preservation of the other.

  "These considerations speak a persuasive language
to every reflecting and virtuous mind; and exhibit
the continuance of the UNION as a primary object of
patriotic desire. Is there a doubt, whether a common
government can embrace so large a sphere. Let

experience solve it. To listen to mere speculation in such a case were criminal. We are authorised to hope that a proper organization of the whole, with the auxiliary agency of governments for the respective subdivisions, will afford a happy issue to the experiment. 'Tis well worth a fair and full experiment. With such powerful and obvious motives to union, affecting all parts of our country, while experience shall not have demonstrated its impracticability, there will always be reason to distrust the patriotism of those, who in any quarter may endeavor to weaken its bands.

"In contemplating the causes which may disturb our union, it occurs, as a matter of serious concern, that any ground should have been furnished for characterizing parties by geographical discriminations—northern and southern—atlantic and western; whence designing men may endeavor to excite a belief, that there is a real difference of local interests and views. One of the expedients of party to acquire influence, within particular districts, is to misrepresent the opinions and aims of other districts. You cannot shield yourselves too much against the jealousies and heart-burnings which spring from these misrepresentations. They tend to render alien to each other, those who ought to be bound together by fraternal affection. The inhabitants of our western country have lately had a useful lesson on this head. They have seen, in the negociation by the executive, and in the unanimous ratification by the senate, of the treaty with Spain, and in the universal satisfaction at that event throughout the United States, a decisive proof how unfounded were the suspicions propagated among them, of a policy in the general government, and in the Atlantic States, unfriendly to their interest in regard to the Mississippi. They have been witnesses to the formation of two treaties, that with Great-Britain, and that with Spain, which secure to them every thing they could desire, in respect to our foreign relations, towards confirming. their posterity. Will it not be their wisdom to rely for the preservation of these advantages on the union by which they were procured? Will they not henceforth be deaf to those advisers, if such there are, who would sever from them their brethren, and connect them with aliens?

"To the efficacy and permanency of your union, a government for the whole is indispensable. No alliances, however strict, between the parts, can be an adequate substitute. They must inevitably experience the infractions and interruptions which all alliances in all times have experienced. Sensible of this momentous truth, you have improved upon your first essay, by the adoption of a constitution of government better calculated than your former, for an intimate union, and for the efficacious management of your common concerns. This government, the offspring of your own choice, uninfluenced and unawed, adopted upon full investigation and mature deliberation, completely free in its principles, in the distribution of its powers, uniting security with energy, and containing within itself a provision for its own amendment, has a just claim to your confidence and your support. Respect for its authority, compliance with its laws, acquiescence in its measures, are duties enjoined by the fundamental maxims of true liberty. The basis of our political systems is the right of the people to make and alter their constitutions of government. But the constitution which at any time exists, till changed by an explicit and authentic act of the whole people, is sacredly obligatory upon all. The very idea of the power and the right of the people to establish government, pre-supposes the duty of every individual to obey the established government.

" All obstructions to the execution of the laws, all combinations and associations, under whatever plausible character, with a real design to direct, control, counteract, or awe the regular deliberation and action of the constituted authorities, are destructive of this fundamental principle, and of fatal tendency. They serve to organize faction; to give it an artificial and extraordinary force; to put in the place of the delegated will of the nation, the will of a party, often a small, but artful and enterprising minority of the community; and, according to the alternate triumphs of different parties, to make the public administration the mirror of the ill-concerted and incongruous projects of faction, rather than the organ of consistent and wholesome plans, digested by common counsels, and modified by mutual interests.

"However combinations or associations of the above description may now and then answer popular ends, they are likely, in the course of time and things, to become potent engines, by which cunning, ambitious, and unprincipled men will be enabled to subvert the power of the people; and to usurp to themselves the reins of government; destroying afterwards the very engines which have lifted them to unjust dominion.

"Towards the preservation of your government, and the permanency of your present happy state, it is requisite, not only that you speedily discountenance irregular oppositions to its acknowledged authority, but also that you resist with care the spirit of innovation upon its principles, however specious the pretexts. One method of assault may be to effect, in the forms of the constitution, alterations which will impair the energy of the system; and thus to undermine what cannot be directly overthrown. In all the changes to which you may be invited, remember that time and habit are at least as necessary to fix the true character of government, as of other human institutions; that experience is the surest standard, by which to test the real tendency of the existing constitution of a country; that facility in changes, upon the credit of mere hypothesis and opinion, exposes to perpetual change, from the endless variety of hypothesis and opinion. And remember, especially, that for the efficient management of your common interests, in a country so extensive as ours, a government of as much vigor as is consistent with the perfect security of liberty, is indispensable. Liberty itself will find in such a government, with powers properly distributed and adjusted, its surest guardian. It is, indeed, little else than a name, where the government is too feeble to withstand the enterprises of faction; to confine each member of the society within the limits prescribed by the laws; and to maintain all in the secure and tranquil enjoyment of the rights of person and property.

"I have already intimated to you the danger of the parties in the state, with particular reference to the founding of them on geographical discriminations. Let me now take a more comprehensive view, and warn you in the most solemn manner against the baneful effects of the spirit of party, generally.

"This spirit, unfortunately, is inseparable from our nature, having its root in the strongest passions of the human mind. It exists under different shapes in all governments, more or less stifled, controlled, or repressed. But in those of the popular form, it is seen in its greatest rankness; and is truly their worst enemy.

"The alternate dominion of one faction over another, sharpened by the spirit of revenge natural to party dissention, which, in different ages and countries, has perpetrated the most horrid enormities, is itself frightful despotism. But this leads at length to a formal and permanent despotism. The disorders and miseries which result, gradually incline the minds of men to seek security and repose in the absolute power of an individual. And, sooner or later, the chief of some prevailing faction, more able or more fortunate than his competitors, turns this disposition to the purposes of his own elevation, on the ruins of public liberty.

"Without looking forward to an extremity of this kind (which, nevertheless, ought not to be entirely out of sight,) the common and continual mischiefs of the spirit of party are sufficient to make it the interest and duty of a wise people to discourage and restrain it.

"It serves always to distract the public councils, and enfeeble the public administration. It agitates the community with ill founded jealousies and false alarms; kindles the animosity of one part against another; foments occasionally riot and insurrection; and opens the door to foreign influence and corruption, which find a facilitated access to the government itself through the channels of party passions. Thus the policy and will of one country are subjected to the policy and will of another.

"There is an opinion that parties in free countries are useful checks upon the administration of the government, and serve to keep alive the spirit of liberty. This, within certain limits, is probably true, and, in governments of a monarchical cast, patriotism may look with indulgence, if not with favor, upon the spirit of party. But in those of the popular character, in governments purely elective, it is a spirit not to be encouraged. From their natural tendency, it is certain there will always be enough of this spirit for every salutary purpose. And there being constant danger of excess, the effort ought to be, by force of public opinion, to mitigate and assuage it. A fire not to be quenched, it demands a uniform vigilance to prevent its bursting into a flame, lest, instead of warming, it should consume.

"It is important, likewise, that the habits of thinking in a free country should inspire caution, in those entrusted with its administration, to confine themselves within their respective constitutional spheres, avoiding, in the exercise of the powers of one department, to encroach upon another. The spirit of encroachment tends to consolidate the powers of all the departments in one, and thus to create, whatever the form of government, a real despotism. A just estimate of that love of power, and proneness to abuse it, which predominates in the human heart, is sufficient to satisfy us of the truth of this position. The necessity of reciprocal checks, in the exercise of political power, by dividing and distributing it into different depositories, and constituting each the guardian of public weal against invasions by the others, has been evinced by experiments ancient and modern; some of them in our country, and under our own eyes. To preserve them must be as necessary as to institute them. If, in the opinion of the people, the distribution or modification of the constitutional powers be in any particular wrong, let it be corrected by an amendment in the way which the constitution designates. But let there be no change by usurpation; for though this, in one instance, may be the instrument of good, it is the customary weapon by which free governments are destroyed. The precedent must always greatly overbalance, in permanent evil, any partial or transient benefit which the use can at any time yield.

"Of all the dispositions and habits which lead to political prosperity, religion and morality are indispensable supports. In vain would that man claim the tribute of patriotism, who should labor to subvert these great pillars of human happiness, these firmest props of the duties of men and citizens. The mere politician, equally with the pious man, ought to respect and to cherish them. A volume could not trace all their connexions with private and public felicity. Let it be simply asked, where is the security for property, for reputation, for life, if the sense of religious obligations desert the oaths, which are the instruments of investigation in the courts of justice? And let us with caution indulge the supposition, that morality can be obtained without religion. Whatever may be conceded to the influence of refined education on minds of peculiar structure, reason and ex-

perience both forbid us to expect that national morality can prevail in exclusion of religious principle.

" 'Tis substantially true, that virtue or morality is
a necessary spring of popular government. The rule
indeed extends with more or less force to every spe-
cies of free government. Who that is a sincere
friend to it can look with indifference upon attempts to shake the foundation of the fabric?

" Promote, then, as an object of primary importance, institutions for the general diffusion of knowledge. In proportion as the structure of a government gives force to public opinion, it is essential that
public opinion should be enlightened.

" As a very important source of strength and security, cherish public credit. One method of preserving it, is to use it as sparingly as possible; avoiding
occasions of expense by cultivating peace; but remembering also that timely disbursements to prepare
for danger frequently prevent much greater disbursements to repel it; avoiding likewise the accumula-
tions of debt, not only by shunning occasions of
expense, but by vigorous exertions, in time of peace,
to discharge the debts which unavoidable wars may
have occasioned; not ungenerously throwing upon
posterity the burden which we ourselves ought to
bear. The execution of these maxims belongs to
your representatives; but it is necessary that public
opinion should co-operate. To facilitate to them the
performance of their duty, it is essential that you
should practically bear in mind, that towards the payment of debts there must be revenue; that to have
revenue there must be taxes; that no taxes can be
devised which are not more or less inconvenient and
unpleasant; that the intrinsic embarrassment inseparable from the selection of the proper object (which
is always a choice of difficulties) ought to be a decisive motive for a candid construction of the conduct
of the government in making it, and for a spirit of

15

acquiescence in the measures for obtaining revenue, which the public exigencies may at any time dictate.

"Observe good faith and justice towards all nations; cultivate peace and harmony with all. Religion and morality enjoin this conduct: and can it be that good policy does not equally enjoin it? It will be worthy of a free, enlightened, and at no distant period a great nation, to give to mankind the magnanimous and too novel example of a people always guided by an exalted justice and benevolence. Who can doubt that in the course of time and things, the fruits of such a plan would richly repay any temporary advantages which might be lost by a steady adherence to it. Can it be, that Providence has not connected the permanent felicity of a nation with its virtue? The experiment, at least, is recommended by every sentiment which ennobles human nature. Alas! is it rendered impossible by its vices?

"In the execution of such a plan, nothing is more essential than that permanent, inveterate antipathies against particular nations, and passionate attachments for others, should be excluded; and that in place of them just and amicable feelings towards all should be cultivated. The nation which indulges towards another an habitual hatred, or an habitual fondness, is in some degree a slave. It is a slave to its animosity or to its affection, either of which is sufficient to lead it astray from its duty and its interest. Antipathy in one nation against another disposes each more readily to offer insult and injury; to lay hold of slight causes of umbrage; and to be haughty and intractable, when accidental or trifling occasions of dispute occur. Hence frequent collisions, obstinate, envenomed, and bloody contests. The nation, prompted by ill-will and resentment, sometimes impels to war the government, contrary to the best calculations of policy. The government sometimes participates in the national propensity; and adopts, through passion, what reason would reject. At other times, it makes the animosity of the nation subservient to projects of hostility, instigated by pride, ambition, and other sinister and pernicious motives. The peace often, sometimes perhaps the liberty, of nations has been the victim.

"So, likewise, a passionate attachment of one nation for another produces a variety of evils. Sympathy for the favorite nation, facilitating the illusion of an imaginary common interest, in cases where no real common interest exists, and infusing into one the enmities of the other, betrays the former into a participation in the quarrels and wars of the latter, without adequate inducement or justification. It leads also to concessions to the favorite nation, of privileges denied to others, which is apt doubly to injure the nation, making the concessions; by unnecessarily parting with what ought to have been retained; and by exciting jealousy, ill-will, and a disposition to retaliate, in the parties from whom equal privileges are withheld. And it gives to ambitious, corrupted, or deluded citizens (who devote themselves to the favourite nation) facility to betray or sacrifice the interests of their own country, without odium, sometimes even with popularity; gilding, with the appearances of a virtuous sense of obligation, a commendable deference for public opinion, or a laudable zeal for public good, the base or foolish compliances of ambition, corruption, or infatuation.

"As avenues to foreign influence in innumerable ways, such attachments are particularly alarming to the truly enlightened and independent patriot. How many opportunities do they afford to tamper with domestic factions; to practise the arts of seduction; to mislead public opinion; to influence or awe the public councils! Such an attachment of a small or weak, towards a great and powerful nation, dooms the former to be the satellite of the latter.

"Against the insidious wiles of foreign influence (I conjure you to believe me, fellow-citizens) the jealousy of a free people ought to be CONSTANTLY awake; since history and experience prove that foreign influence is one of the most baneful foes of republican government. But that jealousy, to be useful, must be impartial; else it becomes the instrument of the very influence to be avoided, instead of a defence against it. Excessive partiality for one foreign nation, and excessive dislike of another, cause, those whom they actuate, to see danger only on one side; and serve to veil and even second the arts of influence on the other. Real patriots, who may resist the intrigues of the favorite, are liable to become suspected and odious, while its fools and dupes usurp the applause and confidence of the people, to surrender their interests.

"The great rule of conduct for us, in regard to foreign nations, is, in extending our commercial relations, to have with them as little POLITICAL connexion as possible. So far as we have already formed engagements, let them be fulfilled with perfect good faith. Here let us stop.

"Europe has a set of primary interests, which to us have none, or a very remote relation. Hence she must be engaged in frequent controversies, the causes of which are essentially foreign to our concerns. Hence, therefore, it must be unwise in us to implicate ourselves, by artificial ties, in the ordinary vicissitudes of her politics, or the ordinary combinations and collisions of her friendships or enmities.

"Our detached and distant situation invites and enables us to pursue a different course. If we remain one people, under an efficient government, the period is not far off, when we may defy material injury from external annoyance; when we may take such an attitude as will cause the neutrality, we may at any time resolve upon, to be scrupulously respected; when belligerent nations, under the impossibility of making acquisitions upon us, will not lightly hazard the giving us provocations; when we may choose peace or war, as our interest, guided by justice, shall counsel.

"Why forego the advantages of so peculiar a situation? Why quit our own, to stand upon foreign ground? Why, by interweaving our destiny with that of any part of Europe, entangle our peace and prosperity in the toils of European ambition, rivalship, interest, humour, or caprice?

" 'Tis our true policy to steer clear of permanent alliances, with any portion of the foreign world; so far, I mean, as we are now at liberty to do it; for let me not be understood as capable of patronising infidelity to existing engagements. I hold the maxim no less applicable to public than to private affairs, that honesty is always the best policy. I repeat it, therefore, let those engagements be observed in their genuine sense. But, in my opinion, it is unnecessary, and would be unwise, to extend them.

" Taking care always to keep ourselves, by suitable establishments, in a respectable defensive posture, we may safely trust to temporary alliances for extraordinary emergencies.

"Harmony and a liberal intercourse with all nations, are recommended by policy, humanity, and interest. But even our commercial policy should hold an equal and impartial hand; neither seeking nor granting exclusive favors or preferences; consulting the natural course of things; diffusing and diversifying by gentle means the streams of commerce, but forcing nothing; establishing, (with powers so disposed, in order to give trade a stable course, to define the rights of our merchants, and to enable the government to support them,) conventional rules of intercourse, the best that present circumstances and mutual opinion will permit, but temporary, and liable to be from time to time abandoned or varied, as experience and circumstances shall dictate; constantly keeping in view, that it is folly in one nation to look for disinterested favors from another; that it must pay with a portion of its independence, for whatever it may accept under that character; that, by such acceptance, it may place

15*

itself in the condition of having given equivalents for nominal favors, and yet of being reproached with ingratitude for not giving more. There can be no greater error than to expect or calculate upon real favors from nation to nation. It is an illusion which experience must cure, which a just pride ought to discard.

" In offering to you, my countrymen, these counsels of an old and affectionate friend, I dare not hope they will make the strong and lasting impression I could wish; that they will control the usual current of the passions, or prevent our nation from running the course which has hitherto marked the destiny of nations! but, if I may even flatter myself, that they may be productive of some partial benefit, some occasional good; that they may now and then recur to moderate the fury of party spirit; to warn against the mischiefs of foreign intrigue; to guard against the impostures of pretended patriotism; this hope will be a full recompense for the solicitude for your welfare, by which they have been dictated.

" How far, in the discharge of my official duties, I have been guided by the principles which have been delineated, the public records and other evidences of my conduct must witness to you and to the world. To myself, the assurance of my own conscience is, that I have, at least, believed myself to be guided by them.

" In relation to the still subsisting war in Europe, my proclamation of the 22nd of April, 1793, is the index to my plan. Sanctioned by your approving voice, and by that of your representatives in both houses of congress, the spirit of that measure has continually governed me, uninfluenced by any attempts to deter or divert me from it.

" After deliberate examination, with the aid of the best lights I could obtain, I was well satisfied that our country, under all the circumstances of the case, had a right to take, and was bound in duty and

interest to take, a neutral position. Having taken
it, I determined, as far as should depend upon me, to
maintain it with moderation, perseverance, and firmness.

"The considerations which respect the right to
hold this conduct, it is not necessary on this occasion
to detail. I will only observe, that according to my
understanding of the matter, that right, so far from
being denied by any of the belligerent powers, has
been virtually admitted by all.

"The duty of holding a neutral conduct may be
inferred, without any thing more, from the obligation
which justice and humanity impose on every nation,
in cases in which it is free to act, to maintain in-
violate the relations of peace and amity towards other
nations.

"The inducements of interest for observing that
conduct will best be referred to your own reflections
and experience. With me, a predominant motive
has been, to endeavour to gain time to our country
to settle and mature its yet recent institutions, and
to progress without interruption to that degree of
strength and consistency, which is necessary to give
it, humanly speaking, the command of its own
fortunes.

"Though, in reviewing the incidents of my
administration, I am unconscious of intentional
error, I am nevertheless too sensible of my defects,
not to think it probable that I may have committed
many errors. Whatever they may be, I fervently
beseech the Almighty to avert or mitigate the evils
to which they may tend. I shall also carry with me
the hope that my country will never cease to view
them with indulgence; and that, after forty-five years
of my life dedicated to its service, with an upright
zeal, the faults of incompetent abilities will be consigned to oblivion, as myself must soon be to the
mansions of rest.

"Relying on its kindness in this as in other things,

and actuated by that fervent love towards it, which is so natural to a man, who views in it the native soil of himself and his progenitors for several generations, I anticipate with pleasing expectation that retreat, in which I promise myself to realize, without alloy, the sweet enjoyment of partaking, in the midst of my fellow citizens, the benign influence of good laws under a free government—the ever favourite object of my heart, and the happy reward, as I trust, of our mutual cause, labours and dangers.

G. WASHINGTON.

" *United States,*
  27th Sept., 1796."

The appearance of this address in the gazettes of the United States, struck every where a damp on the spirits of the people. To be thus bidden farewell by one to whom, in every time of danger, they had so long and so fondly looked up, as, under God, their surest and safest friend, could not but prove to them a grievous shock. Indeed many could not refrain from tears, especially when they came to that part where he talked of being soon to be "consigned to the mansions of rest."

During the next and last session that he ever met congress, which began on the 7th of December, 1796, he laboured hard to induce that honourable body instantly to set about the following public works, which, to him, appeared all important to the nation.

1st. Societies and institutions for the improvement of agriculture.

2d. A navy.

3d. A military Academy.

4th. A manufactory of arms.

5th. A national university.

On the 4th of March, 1797, he took his last leave of Philadelphia. Having ever been an enlightened and virtuous republican, who deems it the first of duties to honour the man whom the majority of his countrymen had chosen to honour, Washington could not think of going away, until he had first paid his respects to the man of their choice. It was this that retarded his journey—it was this that brought him to the senate chamber.

About eleven o'clock, while the members of congress, with numbers of the first characters, were assembled in the senate hall, anxiously awaiting the arrival of Mr. Adams, a modest rap was heard at the door. Supposing it to be the president elect, the attention of all was turned to the entry, when, lo! instead of Mr. Adams and his suite, who should appear but the honoured and beloved form of Washington, without attendants, and in his plain travelling dress. Instantly the joy of filial love sprung up in all hearts, glowed in every face; and bursted forth in involuntary plaudits from every tongue. Presently Mr. Adams entered with his attendants; but passed on in a great measure unnoticed. The father of his country was in the presence of his children, and perhaps for the last time; who then could divide his attentions. Riveted on his face was every glistening eye; while busy memory, flying over the many toils and dangers of his patriot life, gave the spectators up to those delicious thoughts from which no obtruder could break them without a sigh.

Having just waited to congratulate Mr. Adams on his inauguration, and very heartily to pray that "his government might prove a great joy to himself and a blessing to his country," he hastened to Mount Vernon; to close in peace the short evening of this laborious life; and to wait for a better, even for that "rest which remaineth for the people of God."

He carried with him the most fervent prayers of congress, that "Heaven would pour its happiest sunshine on the decline of his days." But this their prayer was not fully answered. On the contrary, with respect to his country, at least, his evening sun went down under a cloud.

The French directory, engaged in a furious war with England, turned to America for aid. But Washington, wisely dreading the effects of war on his young repubiic, and believing that she had an unquestioned right to neutrality, most strictly injoined it on his people by proclamation. This so enraged the directory, that they presently gave orders to theii cruizers, to seize American ships on the high seas—that equal path which God had spread for the nations to trade on! Washington had sent out genèral Charles C. Pinckney to remonstrate against such iniquitous proceedings. The directory would not receive him! but still continued their spoliations on our wide-spread and defenceless commerce, ruining numbers of innocent families. Still determined, according to Washington's advice, "so to act as to put our enemy in the wrong," the American government dispatched two other envoys, Gen. Marshall and Elbridge Gerry, to aid Pinckney. But they fared no better. Though they only supplicated for peace; though they only prayed to be permitted to make explanations, they were still kept by the directory at a most mortifying distance; and, after all, were told, that America was not to look for a single smile of reconciliation, nor even a word on that subject, until her envoys should bring large tribute in their hands!! This, as Washington had predicted, instantly evaporated the last drop of American patience. He had always said, that "though some very interested or deluded persons were much too fond of England and France to value America as they ought; yet he was firmly persuaded, that the great mass of the people were hearty lovers of their country; and, as soon as their eyes were open to the grievous injuries done her, would assuredly resent them, like men, to whom God had given strong feelings, on purpose to guard their rights."

His prediction was gloriously verified. For, on hearing the word tribute, the American envoys instantly took fire!! while the brave Gen. Pinckney, (a revolutionary soldier, and neither Englishman nor Frenchman, but a true American,) indignantly exclaimed to the secretary of the directory—"Tribute, sir! no, sir! the Americans pay no tribute! tell the directory, that we will give millions for defence, but not a cent for tribute."

Soon as this demand of the directory was told in America, the glorious spirit of '76 was kindled like a flash of lightning, from St. Mary's to Maine. "What!" said the people every where, "shall we, shall Americans! who, rather than pay an unconstitutional three-penny tax on tea, bravely encountered a bloody war with Britain, now tamely yield to France to beggar us at pleasure? No! Millions for defence, but not a cent for tribute," was nobly reverberated throughout the continent.

War being now fully expected, the eyes of the nation were instantly turned towards Washington, to head her armies against the French. He readily consented; but, at the same time, observed that there would be no war. "The directory," said he, "though mad enough to do almost any thing, are yet not quite so mad as to venture an attack, when they shall find that the spirit of the nation is up." The event showed the usual correctness of his judgment; for, on discovering that America, though very willing to be the sister, had no notion of being the slave of France—on learning that Washington was roused, and the strength of the nation rallying around him—and also that the American tars, led on by the gallant Truxton, had spread the fiery stars of liberty, blasting on every sea the sickly fleurs-de-luce, of gallic piracy, the directory very sagaciously signified a disposition to accommodate. Mr. Adams immediately despatched three new envoys to the French republic. By the time they got there, the French republic was no more! Bonaparte, believing that volatile people incapable of governing for themselves, had kindly, undertaken to govern for them; and having, en passant, kicked the directory from their seats, he seized their ill-managed power, and very leisurely mounted the throne of the Bourbons. Dazzled with, the splendor of his talents and victories, the great nation quietly yielded to his reign; and with a happy versatility peculiar to themselves, exchanged the tumultuous and bloody "Caira," for the milder notes of "vive l'empereur." With this wonderful man, the American envoys found no difficulty to negotiate; for having no wish to re-unite America to his hated. enemy, Britain, he received them very graciously; and presently settled all their claims in a satisfactory manner. Thus lovingly did the breath of God blow, away once more the black cloud of war, and restore the bright day of peace to our favoured land! But, Washington never lived to rejoice with his country-men in the sunshine of that peace; for before it reached our shores, he had closed his eyes for ever on all mortal things.

CHAPTER XII.

THE DEATH OF WASHINGTON,

And when disease obstructs the labouring breath,
When the heart sickens and each pulse is death,
Even then Religion shall sustain the just;
Grace their last moments; nor desert their dust.

If the prayers of millions could have prevailed, Washington would have been immortal on earth. And if fulness of peace, riches, and honours could. have rendered that immortality happy, Washington had been blessed indeed. But this world is not the place of true happiness. Though numberless are the satisfactions, which a prudence and virtue like Wash-

ington's may enjoy in this world, yet they fall short,
infinite degrees, of that pure, unembittered felicity
which the Almighty parent has prepared in heaven
for the spirits of the just.

To prepare for this immensity of bliss, is the real
errand on which God sent us into the world. Our
preparation consists in acquiring those great virtues,
purity and love, which alone can make us worthy
companions of angels, and fit partakers of their exalted delights. Washington had wisely spent his life
in acquiring the immortal virtues. "He had fought
the good fight" against his own unreasonable affections. He had glorified God, by exemplifying the
charms of virtue to men. He had borne the heat
and burden of the day—his great day of duty: and
the evening of old age being come, the servant of God
must now go to receive his wages. Happy Washington! If crowns and kingdoms could have purchas-
ed such peace as thine, such hopes big with immortality, with what begging earnestness would crowns
and kingdoms have been offered by the mighty conquerors of the earth, in their dying moments of terror
and despair!

On the 14th of December, 1799, (when he wanted
but nine weeks and two days of being sixty-eight
years old,) he rode out to his mill, three miles distant.
The day was raw and rainy. The following night
he was attacked with a violent pain and inflammation of the throat. The lancet of one of his domestics
was employed, but with no advantage. Early in the
morning, Dr. Craik, the friend and physician of his
youth and age, was sent for. Alarmed at the least
appearance of danger threatening a life so dear to
him, Dr. Craik advised to call in, immediately, the
consulting assistance of his friends, the ingenious and
learned Dr. Dick, of Alexandria, and Dr. Brown, of
Port Tobacco. They came on the wings of speed.
They felt the awfulness of their situation. The
greatest of human beings was lying low. A life, of

16

all others the most revered, the most beloved, was at stake. And if human skill could have saved—if the sword of genius, and the buckler of experience could have turned the stroke of death, Washington had still lived. But his hour was come.

It appears, that from the commencement of the attack, he was favored with a presentiment, that he was now laid down to rise no more. He took, however, the medicines that were offered him: but it was principally from a sense of duty.

It has been said that a man's death is generally a copy of his life. It was Washington's case exactly. In his last illness he behaved with the firmness of a soldier, and the resignation of a christian.

The inflammation in his throat was attended with great pain, which he bore with the fortitude that became him. He was, once or twice, heard to say that, had it pleased God, he should have been glad to die a little easier; but that he doubted not that it was for his good.

Every hour now spread a sadder gloom over the scene. Despair sat on the faces of the physicians; for they saw that their art had failed! The strength of the mighty was departing from him; and death, with his sad harbingers, chills and paleness, was coming on apace.

Mount Vernon, which had long shone the queen of elegant joys, was now about to suffer a sad eclipse! an eclipse, which would soon be mournfully visible, not only through the United States, but throughout the whole world.

Sons and daughters of Columbia, gather yourselves together around the bed of your expiring father— around the last bed of him to whom under God you and your children owe many of the best blessings of this life. When Joseph the prime minister of Egypt heard that his shepherd father was sick, he hastened up, to see him; and fell on his face, and kissed him, and wept a long while. But Joseph had never received such services from Jacob as you have received from Washington. But we call you not to weep for Washington. We ask you not to view those eyes, now sunk hollow, which formerly darted their lightning flashes against your enemies—nor to feel that heart, now faintly laboring, which so often throbbed with more than mortal joys when he saw his young countrymen charging like lions, upon the foes of liberty. No! we call you not to weep, but to rejoice. Washington, who so often conquered himself, is now about to conquer the last enemy.

Silent and sad his physicians sat by his bedside, looking on him as he lay panting for breath. They thought on the past, and the tear swelled in their eyes. He marked it, and, stretching out his hand to them, and shaking his head, said, "O no! don't! don't!" then with a delightful smile added, "I am dying, gentlemen! but, thank God, I am not afraid to die."

Feeling that the hour of his departure out of this world was at hand, he desired that every body would quit the room. They all went out; and, according to his wish, left him—with his God.

There, by himself, like Moses alone on the top of Pisgah, he seeks the face of God. There, by himself, standing as on the awful boundary that divides time from eternity, that separates this world from the next, he cannot quit the long frequented haunts of the one, nor launch away into the untried regions of the other, until (in humble imitation of the world's great Redeemer,) he has poured forth, into the bosom of his God, those strong sensations which the solemnity of his situation naturally suggested.

With what angelic fervor did he adore that Almighty Love, which, though inhabiting the heaven of heavens, deigned to wake his sleeping dust—framed him so fearfully in the womb—nursed him on a tender mother's breast—watched his helpless infancy—guarded his heedless youth—preserved him

from the dominion of his passions—inspired him with
the love of virtue—led him safely up to man—and,
from such low beginnings, advanced him to such
unparalleled usefulness and glory among men!
These, and ten thousand other precious gifts heaped
on him, unasked—many of them long before he had
the knowledge to ask—overwhelmed his soul with
gratitude unutterable; exalted to infinite heights his
ideas of eternal love; and bade him without fear
resign his departing spirit into the arms of his
Redeemer God, whose mercies are over all his
works.

He is now about to leave the great family of man,
in which he has so long sojourned! The yearnings
of his soul are over his brethren! How fervently
does he adore that goodness, which enabled him to
be so serviceable to them! that grace, which preserved him from injuring them by violence or fraud!
How fervently does he pray, that the unsuffering
kingdom of God may come, and that the earth may
be filled with the richest fruits of righteousness and
peace!

He is now about to leave his country! that dear
spot which gave him birth—that dear spot for which
he has so long watched and prayed, so long toiled
and fought; and whose beloved children he has so
often sought to gather, "even as a hen gathereth her
chickens under her wings." He sees them now
spread abroad like flocks in goodly pastures; like
favoured Israel in the land of promise. He remem-
bers how God, by a mighty hand, and by an out-
stretched arm, brought their fathers into this good
land, a land flowing with milk and honey; and
blessed them with the blessings of heaven above, and
the earth beneath; with the blessings of liberty and
of peace, of religion and of laws, above all other
people. He sees that, through the rich mercies of
God, they have now the precious opportunity to
continue their country the glory of the earth, and a

refuge for the poor, and for the persecuted of all lands! The transporting sight of such a cloud of blessings, impending close over the heads of his countrymen, together with the distressing uncertainty whether they will put forth their hands and enjoy them, shakes the parent soul of Washington with feelings too strong for his dying frame! The last tear that he is ever to shed, now steals into his eye —the last groan that he is ever to heave, is about to issue from his faintly labouring heart.

Feeling that the silver cord of life is loosing, and that his spirit is ready to quit her old companion, the body, he extends himself on his bed—closes his eyes for the last time with his own hands—folds his arms decently on his breast, then breathing out "Father of mercies, take me to thyself,"—he fell asleep.

Swift on angel's wings the brightening saint ascended; while voices more than human were warbling through the happy regions, and hymning the great procession towards the gates of heaven. His glorious coming was seen afar off; and myriads of mighty angels hastened forth, with golden harps, to welcome the honoured stranger. High in front of the shouting hosts, were seen the beauteous forms of Franklin, Warren, Mercer, Scammel, and of him who fell at Quebec, with all the virtuous patriots, who, on the side of Columbia, toiled or bled for liberty and truth. But oh! how changed from what they were, when, in their days of flesh, bathed in sweat and blood, they fell at the parent feet of their weeping country! Not the homeliest infant suddenly spring-ing into a soul-enchanting Hebe—not dreary winter suddenly brightening into spring, with all her bloom and fragrance, ravishing the senses, could equal such a glorious change. Oh! where are now their wrinkles and grey hairs? Where their ghastly wounds and clotted blood? Their forms are of the stature of angels—their robes like morning clouds streaked with gold—the stars of heaven, like crowns,

16*

glitter on their heads—immortal youth, celestial **rosy** red, sits blooming on their cheeks, while infinite benignity and love beam from their eyes.   Such were the forms of thy sons, O Columbia! such the brother band of thy martyred saints, that now poured forth from heaven's wide opening gates, to meet thy Washington; to meet their beloved chief, who, in the days of his mortality, had led their embattled squadrons to the war.   At sight of him, even these blessed spirits seem to feel new raptures, and to look more dazzlingly bright.   In joyous throngs they pour around him—they devour him with their eyes of love —they embrace him in transports of tenderness unutterable; while from their roseate cheeks, tears of joy, such as angels weep, roll down.

All that followed was too much for the overdazzled eye of imagination.   She was seen to return, with the quick panting bosom and looks entranced of a fond mother, near swooning at sudden sight of a dear loved son, deemed lost, but now found, and raised to kingly honours!   She was heard passionately to exclaim, with palms and eyes lifted to heaven, "O, who can count the stars of Jacob, or number the fourth part of the blessings of Israel!— Let me die the death of Washington! and may my latter end be like his!"

Let us now return to all that remained of Washington on earth.   He had expressly ordered in his will, that he should be buried in a private manner, and without any parade.   But this was impossible; for who could stay at home when it was said, "To-day General Washington is to be buried!"   On the morning of the 18th, which was fixed on for his funeral, the people poured in by thousands to pay him the last respect, and, as they said, to take their last look.   And, while they looked on him, nature stirred that at their hearts, which quickly brought the best blood into their cheeks, and rolled down the tears from their eyes.   About two o'clock they bore him to his long home, and buried him in his own family vault, near the banks of the great Potomac. And to this day, often as the ships of war pass that way, they waken up the thunder of their loudest guns, pointed to the spot, as if to tell the sleeping hero, that he is not forgotten in his narrow dwelling.

The news of his death soon reached Philadelphia, where Congress was then in session. A question of importance being on the carpet that day, the house, as usual, was much interested. But soon as it was announced—"General Washington is dead"—an instant stop was put to all business—the tongue of the orator was struck dumb—and a midnight silence ensued, save when it was interrupted by deepest sighs of the members, as, with drooping foreheads rested on their palms, they sat, each absorbed in mournful cogitation. Presently, as utterly unfit for business, both houses adjourned; and the members retired slow and sad to their lodgings, like men who had suddenly heard of the death of a father.

For several days hardly any thing was done in Congress; hardly any thing thought of but to talk of and to praise the departed Washington. In this patriotic work all parties joined with equal alacrity and earnestness. In this all were federalists, all were republicans. Elegant addresses were exchanged between the two houses of Congress and the President, and all of them replete with genius and gratitude.

Then, by unanimous consent, Congress came to the following resolutions :

1st. That a grand marble monument should be erected at the city of Washington, under which with permission of his lady, the body of the General should be deposited.

2d. That there should be a funeral procession from congress hall to the German Lutheran church, to hear an oration delivered by one of the members of congress.

3d. That the members of congress should wear full mourning during the session.

4th. That it should be recommended to the people of the United States to wear crape on the left arm, as mourning, for thirty days.

But, thank God, the people of the United States needed not the hint contained in the last resolution. Though they could not all very elegantly speak, yet their actions showed that they all very deeply felt what they owed to Washington. For, in every city, village, and hamlet, the people were so struck on hearing of his death, that long before they heard of the resolution of congress, they ran together to ease their troubled minds in talking and hearing talk of Washington, and to devise some public mode of testifying their sorrow for his death. Every where throughout the continent, churches and court houses were hung in black, mourning was put on, processions were made, and sermons preached, while the crowded houses listened with pleasure to the praises of Washington, or sighed and wept when they heard of his toils and battles for his country.

CHAPTER XIII.

CHARACTER OF WASHINGTON.

Let the poor witling argue all he can
It is religion still that makes the man.

WHEN the children of years to come, hearing his great name re-echoed from every lip, shall say to their fathers, " What was it that raised Washington to such a height of glory ?" let them be told that it WAS HIS GREAT TALENTS, CONSTANTLY GUIDED AND GUARDED BY RELIGION. For how shall man, frail man, prone to inglorious ease and pleasure, ever ascend the arduous steps of virtue, unless animated by the mighty hopes of religion ? Or what shall stop him in his swift descent to infamy and vice, if un-awed by that dread power, which proclaims to the guilty that their secret crimes are seen, and shall not go unpunished ? Hence, the wise, in all ages, have pronounced, that " there never was a truly great man without religion."

There have, indeed, been courageous generals, and cunning statesmen, without religion, but mere courage or cunning, however transcendent, never yet made a great man.

> " Admit that this can conquer, that can cheat
> 'Tis phrase absurd, to call a villain great !
> Who wickedly is wise, or madly brave,
> Is but the more a fool, the more a knave."

No ! to be truly great, a man must have not only great talents, but those talents must be constantly exerted on great, i. e. good actions—and perseveringly too—for if he should turn aside to vice—farewell to his heroism. Hence, when Epaminondas was asked which was the greatest man, himself or Pelopidas? he replied, " wait till we are dead :" meaning that the all of heroism depends on perseverance in great and good actions. But sensual and grovelling as man is, what can incline and elevate him to those things like religion, that divine power, to whom alone it belongs to present those vast and eternal goods and ills which best alarm our fears, enrapture our hopes, inflame the worthiest loves, rouse the truest avarice, and in short, touch every spring and passion of our souls in favour of virtue and noble actions.

Did SHAME restrain Alcibiades from a base action in the presence of Socrates? " Behold," says Religion, " a greater than Socrates is here !"

Did LOVE embolden Jacob to brave fourteen years of slavery for an earthly beauty? Religion springs that eternal love, for whose sake good men can even glory in laborious duties.

Did the ambition of a civic crown animate Scipio to heroic deeds? Religion holds a crown, at the sight of which the laurels of a Cæsar droop to weeds.

Did avarice urge Cortez through a thousand toils and dangers for wealth? Religion points to those treasures in heaven, compared to which all diamond beds and mines of massy gold are but trash.

Did good Aurelius study the happiness of his subjects for this world's glory? Religion displays that world of glory, where those who have laboured to make others happy, shall "shine like stars for ever and for ever."

Does the FEAR of death deter man from horrid crimes? Religion adds infinite horrors to that fear—it warns them of death both of soul and body in hell.

In short, what motives under heaven can restrain men from vices and crimes, and urge them on, full stretch, after individual and national happiness, like those of religion? For lack of these motives, alas! how many who once dazzled the world with the glare of their exploits, are now eclipsed and set to rise no more!

There was Arnold, who, in courage and military talents, glittered in the same firmament with Washington, and, for a while, his face shone like the star of the morning; but alas! for lack of Washington's religion, he soon fell, like Lucifer, from a heaven of glory, into an abyss of never ending infamy.

And there was general Charles Lee, too, confessedly a great wit, a great scholar, a great soldier, but, after all, not a great man. For, through lack of that magnanimous benevolence which religion inspires, he fell into the vile state of envy: and, on the plains of Monmouth, rather than fight to immortalize Washington, he chose to retreat and disgrace himself.

There was the gallant general Hamilton also—a gigantic genius—a statesman fit to rule the mightiest monarchy—a soldier "fit to stand by Washington and give command." But alas! for lack of religion, see how all was lost ! preferring the praise of man to that praise " which cometh from God," and pursuing the phantom honour up to the pistol's mouth, he is cut off at once from life and greatness, and leaves his family and country to mourn his hapless fate.

And there was the fascinating colonel Burr, a man born to be great—brave as Cæsar, polished as Chesterfield, eloquent as Cicero. Lifted by the strong arm of his country, he rose fast, and bade fair soon to fill the place where Washington had sat. But alas! lacking religion, he could not wait the spontaneous fall of the rich honors ripening over his head, but in an evil hour stretched forth his hand to the forbidden fruit, and by that fatal act was cast out from the Eden of our republic, and amerced of greatness for ever.

But why should I summon the Arnolds and Lees, the Hamiltons and Burrs of the earth, to give sad evidence, that no valour, no genius alone can make men great ? Do we not daily meet with instances, of youth amiable and promising as their fond parents' wishes, who yet, merely for lack of religion, soon make shipwreck of every precious hope, sacrificing their gold to gamblers, their health to harlots, and their glory to grog—making conscience their curse, this life a purgatory, and the next a hell ! In fact, a young man, though of the finest talents and education, without religion, is but like a gorgeous ship without ballast. Highly painted, and with flowing canvass, she launches out on the deep ; and during a smooth sea and gentle breeze, she moves along stately as the pride of the ocean ; but as soon as the stormy winds descend, and the blackening billows begin to roll, suddenly she is overset, and disappears for ever. But who is this coming thus gloriously along, with masts towering to heaven, and his sails white, looming like the mountain of snows ? Who is it but " Columbia's first and greatest son !" whose talents, like the sails of a mighty ship, spread far and wide, catching the gales of heaven, while his capacious soul, stored with the rich ballast of religion, remains firm and unshaken as the ponderous rock. The warm zephyrs of prosperity breathe meltingly upon him—the rough storms of adversity descend—the big billows of affliction dash : but nothing can move him. His eye is fixed on God ! the present joys of an approving conscience, and the hope of that glory which fadeth not away—these comfort and support him.

"There exists," says Washington, "in the economy of nature, an inseparable connexion between duty and advantage,"—the whole life of this great man bears glorious witness to the truth of this his favorite aphorism. 'At the giddy age of fourteen, when the spirits of youth are all on tiptoe for freedom and adventures, he felt a strong desire to go to sea : but, very opposite to his wishes, his mother declared that she could not bear to part with him. His trial must have been very severe ; for I have been told that a midshipman's commission was actually in his pocket—his trunk of clothes on board the ship—his honour in some sort pledged—his young companions importunate with him to go—and his whole soul panting for the promised pleasures of the voyage. But religion whispered " honour thy mother, and grieve not the spirit of her who bore thee."

Instantly the glorious boy sacrificed inclination to duty—dropt all thought of the voyage—and gave tears of joy to his widowed mother, in clasping to her bosom a dear child who could deny himself his fondest wishes to make her happy.

'Tis said, that when he saw the last boat going on board, with several of his youthful friends in it—when he saw the flash, and heard the report of the signal gun for sailing, and the ship in all her pride of canvass rounding off for sea, he could not bear it ; but turned away ; and half choked with grief, went into the room where his mother sat. " George, my dear !" said she, " have you already repented that you

made your mother so happy just now ?" Upon this,
falling on her bosom, with his arms around her neck,
and a gush of tears, he said : "my dear mother, I
must not deny that I am sorry. But, indeed, I feel
that I should be much more sorry, were I on board
the ship, and knew that you were unhappy."

"Well," replied she, embracing him tenderly, "God,
I hope, will reward my dear boy for this,—some day
or other." Now see here, young reader ; and learn
that HE who prescribes our duty, is able to reward it.
Had George left his fond mother to a broken heart,
and gone off to sea, 'tis next to certain that he would
never have taken that active part in the French and
Indian war, which, by securing him the hearts of his
countrymen, paved the way for all his future greatness.

Now for another instance of the wonderful effect
of religion on Washington's fortune. Shortly after
returning from the war of Cuba, Lawrence (his half
brother) was taken with the consumption, which
made him so excessively fretful, that his own brother
Augustin would seldom come near him. But George,
whose heart was early under the softening and sweet-
ening influences of religion, felt such a tenderness for
his poor sick brother, that he not only submitted to
his peevishness, but seemed, from what I have been
told, never so happy as when he was with him. He
accompanied him to the Island of Bermuda, in quest
of health—and, after their return to Mount Vernon,
as often as his duty to lord Fairfax permitted, he
would come down from the back woods to see him.
And, while with him, he was always contriving or
doing something to cheer and comfort his brother.
Sometimes with his gun he would go out in quest of
partridges and snipes, and other fine-flavored game,
to tempt his brother's sickly appetite, and gain him
strength. At other times he would sit for hours and
read to him some entertaining book : and, when his
cough came on, he would support his drooping head,

17

and wipe the cold dew from his forehead, or the phlegm from his lips, and give him his medicine, or smooth his pillow, and all with such alacrity and artless tenderness as proved the sweetest cordial to his brother's spirits. For he was often heard to say to the Fairfax family, into which he married, that "he should think nothing of his sickness, if he could but always have his brother George with him." Well, what was the consequence? Why, when Lawrence was dying, he left almost the whole of his large estate to George, which served as another noble step to his future greatness.

For further proof of "the inseparable connexion between duty and advantage," let us look at Washington's conduct through the French and Indian war. To a man of his uncommon military mind, and skill in the arts of Indian warfare, the pride and precipitance of general Braddock must have been excessively disgusting and disheartening. But we hear nothing of his threatening either to leave or supplant Braddock. On the contrary, he nobly brooked his rude manners; gallantly obeyed his rash orders; and, as far as in him lay, endeavoured to correct their fatal tendencies.

And, after the death of Braddock, and the desertion of Dunbar, that weak old man, governor Dinwiddie, added infinitely to his hardships and hazards, by appointing him to the defence of the frontiers, and yet withholding the necessary forces and supplies. But though by that means the western country was continually overrun by the enemy, and cruelly deluge in blood—though much wearied in body by marchings and watchings, and worse tortured in soul, by the murders and desolations of the inhabitants, he shrinks not from duty—still seeking the smiles of conscience as his greatest good; and as the sorest evil, dreading its frowns, he bravely maintained his ground, and, after three years of unequalled dangers and difficulties, succeeded.

Well, what was the consequence? why it drew upon him, from his admiring countrymen, such an unbounded confidence in his principles and patriotism, as secured him the command of the American armies, in the revolutionary war!

And there again the connexion between "duty and advantage," was as gloriously displayed. For though congress was, in legal and political knowledge, an enlightened body, and for patriotism equal to the senate of Republican Rome, yet certainly in military matters they were no more to be compared to him, than those others were to Hannibal. But still, though they were constantly thwarting his counsels, and, in place of good soldiers, sending him raw militia, thus compelling inactivity, or insuring defeat—dragging out the war—dispiriting the nation—and disgracing him, yet we hear from him no gusts of passion—no dark intrigues to supplant congress—and with the help of an idolizing nation and army, to snatch the power from their hands, and make himself king. On the contrary, he continues to treat congress as a virtuous son his respected parents. He points out wiser measures, but in defect of their adoption, makes the best use of those they give him, at length, through the mighty blessing of God, established the independence of his country; and then went back to his plough.

Well, what was the consequence? Why, these noble acts so completely filled up the measure of his country's love for him, as to give him that first of all felicities, the felicity to be regarded as the guardian angel of his country, and to be able, by the magic of his name, to scatter every cloud of danger that gathered over her head.

For example, at the close of the war, when the army, about to be disbanded without their wages, were wrought up to such a pitch of discontent and rage, as seriously to threaten civil war, see the wonderful influence which their love for him gave him over themselves! In the height of their passion, **and** that a very natural passion too, he merely makes a short speech to them, and the storm is laid! the tumult subsides! and the soldiers, after all their hardships, consent to ground their arms, and return home without a penny in their pockets!!!

Also, in that very alarming dispute between Vermont and Pennsylvania, when the furious parties, in spite of all the efforts of congress and their governors, had actually shouldered their guns, and were dragging on their cannon for a bloody fight—Washington only gave them a few lines of his advice, and they instantly faced about for their homes; and laying by their weapons, seized their ploughs again, like dutiful children, on whose kindling passions a beloved father had shaken his hoary locks!!

And, in the western counties of Pennsylvania, where certain blind patriots affecting to strain at the gnat of a small excise, but ready enough to swallow the infernal camel of rebellion, had kindled the flames of civil war, and thrown the whole nation into a tremor, Washington had just to send around a circular to the people of the union, stating the infinite importance of maintaining the sacred reign of the laws, and instantly twenty thousand well armed volunteers marched among the insurgents, and, without shedding a drop of blood, extinguished the insurrection.

In short, it were endless to enumerate the many dire insurrections and bloody wars which were averted from this country by Washington, and all through the divine force of early Religion! for it was this that enabled him inflexibly to do his duty, by imitating God in his glorious works of wisdom and benevolence; and all the rest followed as naturally as light follows the sun.

We have seen, at page 17 of this little work, with what pleasure the youthful Washington hung upon his father's lip, while descanting on the adorable wisdom and benevolent designs of God in all parts

of this beautiful and harmonious creation. By such
lessons in the book of nature, this virtuous youth
was easily prepared for the far higher and surer lec-
tures of revelation, I mean that blessed gospel which
contains the moral philosophy of heaven. There
he learnt, that "God is love;"—and that all he de-
sires, with respect to men, is to glorify himself in
their happiness; and since virtue is indispensable to
that happiness, the infinite and eternal weight of
God's attributes must be in favour of virtue, and
against vice; and consequently that God will sooner
or later gloriously reward the one, and punish the
other. This was the creed of Washington. And
looking on it as the only basis of human virtue and
happiness, he very cordially embraced it himself,
and wished for nothing so much as to see all others
embrace it.

I have often been informed by Colonel B. Temple, (of King William County, Virginia,) who was
one of his aids in the French and Indian war, that he
has frequently known Washington, on the Sabbath,
to read scriptures and pray with his regiment, in the
absence of the chaplain; and also that, on sudden and
unexpected visits into his marquee, he has, more than
once, found him on his knees at his devotions.

The Reverend Mr. Lee Massey, long a rector of
Washington's parish, and from early life his intimate,
has frequently assured me, that "he never knew so
constant an attendant on church as Washington.
And his behaviour in the house of God," added my
reverend friend, "was so deeply reverential, that it
produced the happiest effects on my congregation;
and greatly assisted me in my moralizing labours.
No company ever withheld him from church. I
have often been at Mount Vernon, on the Sabbath
morning, when his breakfast table was filled with
guests. But to him they furnished no pretext for
neglecting his God, and losing the satisfaction of
setting a good example. For instead of staying at

home, out of false complaisance to them, he used constantly to invite them to accompany him."

His secretary, Judge Harrison, has frequently been heard to say, that "whenever the general could be spared from camp on the Sabbath, he never failed riding out to some neighbouring church, to join those who were publicly worshipping the great Creator."

And while he resided in Philadelphia, as president of the United States, his constant and cheerful attendance on divine service was such as to convince every reflecting mind, that he deemed no levee so honourable as that of his Almighty Maker; no pleasures equal to those of devotion; and no business a sufficient excuse for neglecting his supreme benefactor.

In the winter of '77, while Washington, with the American army, lay encamped at Valley Forge, a certain good old friend, of the respectable family and name of Potts, if I mistake not, had occasion to pass through the woods near head quarters. Treading in his way along the venerable grove, suddenly he heard the sound of a human voice, which, as he advanced, increased on his ear; and at length became like the voice of one speaking much in earnest. As he approached the spot with a cautious step, whom should he behold, in a dark natural bower of ancient oaks, but the commander in chief of the American armies on his knees at prayer! Motionless with surprise, friend Potts continued on the place till the general, having ended his devotions, arose; and, with a countenance of angelic serenity, retired to headquarters. Friend Potts then went home, and on entering his parlour called out to his wife, "Sarah! my "dear Sarah! all's well! all's well! George Washington will yet prevail!"

"What's the matter, Isaac?" replied she, "thee seems moved."

"Well, if I seem moved, 'tis no more than what I really am. I have this day seen what I never expected. Thee knows that I always thought that the sword and the gospel were utterly inconsistent; and that no man could be a soldier and a christian at the same time. But George Washington has this day convinced me of my mistake."

He then related what he had seen, and concluded with this prophetical remark—"If George Washington be not a man of God, I am greatly deceived—and still more shall I be deceived, if God do not, through him, work out a great salvation for America."

When General Washington was told that the British troops at Lexington, on the memorable 19th of April, 1775, had fired on and killed several of the Americans, he replied, "I grieve for the death of my countrymen; but rejoice that the British are still so determined to keep God on our side," alluding to that noble sentiment which he has since so happily expressed; viz. "The smiles of Heaven can never be expected on a nation that disregards the eternal rules of order and right, which Heaven itself has ordained."

When called by his country in 1775, to lead her free-born sons against the arms of Britain, what charming modesty, what noble self-distrust, what pious confidence in Heaven, appeared in all his answers. "My diffidence in my own abilities," says he, "was superseded by a confidence in the rectitude of our cause, and the patronage of Heaven.'

And when called to the presidency by the unanimous voice of the nation, thanking him for his great services past, with anticipations of equally great to come, his answer deserves approbation.

"When I contemplate the interposition of Providence, as it was visibly manifested in guiding us through the revolution—in preparing us for the reception of a general government—and in conciliating the good will of the people of America towards one another after its adoption; I feel myself oppressed and almost overwhelmed with a sense of the divine munificence. I feel that nothing is due to my

personal agency in all those complicated and wonderful events, except what can simply be attributed
to the exertions of an honest zeal for the good of my
country."

And when he presented himself for the first time
before that august body, the Congress of the United
States, April 30th, 1789—when he saw before him
the pride of Columbia in her chosen sons, assembled
to consult how best to strengthen the chain. of love
between the states—to preserve friendship and harmony with foreign powers—to secure the blessings
of civil and religious liberty—and to build up our
young republic a great and happy people among the
nations of the earth—never patriot entered on such
important business with fairer hopes, whether we
consider the unanimity and confidence of the citizens,
or his own abilities and virtues, and those of his
fellow-counsellors.

But all this would not do. Nothing short of the
divine friendship could satisfy Washington. Feeling
the magnitude, difficulty, and danger of managing
such an assemblage of communities and interests;
dreading the machinations of bad men, and well
knowing the insufficiency of all second causes, even
the best, he piously reminds congress of the wisdom
of imploring the benediction of the great first cause,
without which he knew that his beloved country
would never prosper.

"It would," says he; "be peculiarly improper to
omit, in this first official act, my fervent supplications
to that Almighty Being who rules over the universe;
who presides in the councils of nations; and whose
providential aids can supply every human defect, that
his benediction may consecrate to the liberties and
happiness of the people of the United States, a
government instituted by themselves for these essential purposes; and may enable every instrument
employed in its administration to execute with
success the functions allotted to his charge.   In

tendering this homage to the great Author of every public and private good, I assure myself that it ex-, presses your sentiments not less than my own ; nor those of my fellow citizens at large less than either. No people can be bound to acknowledge and adore the invisible hand which conducts the affairs of men, more than the people of the United States. Every step, by which they have advanced to the character of an independent nation, seems to have been distinguished by some token of providential agency., These reflections, arising out of the present crisis, have forced themselves too strongly on my mind to be suppressed. You will join with me, I trust, in thinking, that there are none, under the influence of which the proceedings of a new and free government can more auspiciously commence."

And after having come near to the close of this, the most sensible and virtuous speech ever made to a sensible and virtuous representation of a free people, he adds—" I shall take my present leave ; but not without resorting once more to the benign Parent of the human race in humble supplication, that, since he has been pleased to favour the American people with opportunities for deliberating with perfect tranquility, and dispositions for deciding with unparalleled unanimity, on a form of government for the security of their union, and the advancement of their happiness ; so his divine blessings may be equally conspicuous in the enlarged views, the temperate consultations, and the wise measures, on which the success of this government must depend."

In this constant disposition to look for national happiness only in national morals, flowing from the sublime affections and blessed hopes of Religion, Washington, agreed with those great legislators of nations, Moses, Lycurgus, and Numa. " I ask not gold for Spartans," said Lycurgus. " Virtue is better than all gold." The event showed his wisdom—

The Spartans were invincible so long as they remained virtuous—even 500 years.

"I ask not wealth for Israel," cried Moses. "But O that they were wise!—that they did but fear God and keep his comandments! The Lord himself would be their sun and shield." The event proved Moses a true prophet. For while they were religious they were unconquerable. "United as brothers, swift as eagles, stronger than lions, one could chase a thousand; and two put ten thousand to flight."

"Of all the dispositions and habits which lead to the prosperity of a nation," says Washington, "Religion is the indispensable support. Volumes could not trace all its connexions with private and public happiness. Let it simply be asked, where is the security for property, for reputation, for life itself, if there be no fear of God on the minds of those who give their oaths in courts of justice."

But some will tell us, that human laws are sufficient for the purpose!

Human laws!—human nonsense! For how often, even where the cries and screams of the wretched called aloud for lightning speeded vengeance, have we not seen the sword of human law loiter in its coward scabbard, afraid of angry royalty? Did not that vile queen Jezebel, having a mind to compliment her husband with a vineyard belonging to poor Naboth, suborn a couple of villians to take a false oath against him; and then cause him to be dragged out with his little motherless, crying babes, and barbarously stoned to death.

Great God! what bloody tragedies have been acted on the poor ones of the earth, by kings and great men, who were above the laws, and had no sense of Religion to keep them in awe! And if men be not above the laws, yet what horrid crimes! what ruinous robberies! what wide-wasting havoc! what cruel murders may they not commit in secret, if they be not withheld by the sacred arm of religion! "In vain, therefore," says Washington, "would that man claim the tribute of patriotism, who should do any thing to discountenance Religion and morality, those great pillars of human happiness, those firmest props of the duties of men and citizens. The mere politician, equally with the pious man, ought to respect and cherish them."

But others have said, and with a serious face too, that a sense of honour is sufficient to preserve men from base actions! O blasphemy to sense! Do we not daily hear of men of honour, by dice and cards, draining their fellow citizens of the last cent, reducing them to beggary; or driving them to a pistol? Do we not daily hear of men of honour corrupting their neighbours wives and daughters, and then murdering the husbands and brothers in duels? Bind such selfish, such inhuman beings, by a sense of honour!! why not bind roaring lions with cobwebs? "No," exclaims Washington, "whatever a sense of honour may do on men of refined education, and on minds of a peculiar structure, reason and experience both forbid us to expect that national morality can prevail in exclusion of Religious principles."

And truly Washington had abundant reason, from his own happy experience, to recommend Religion so heartily to others.

For besides all those inestimable favours which he received from her at the hands of her celestial daughters, the Virtues; she threw over him her own magic mantle of Character. And it was this that immortalized Washington. By inspiring his countrymen with the profoundest veneration for him as the best of men, it naturally smoothed his way to supreme command; so that when War, that monster of satan, came on roaring against America, with all his death's heads and garments rolled in blood, the nation unanimously placed Washington at the head of their armies, from a natural persuasion that so good a man must be the peculiar favourite of Heaven, and the fastest friend of his country. How far this precious instinct in favour of goodness was correct, or how far Washington's conduct was honourable to Religion and glorious to himself and country, bright ages to come, and happy millions yet unborn, will, we confidently hope, declare to the most distant posterity.

CHAPTER XIV.

WASHINGTON'S CHARACTER CONTINUED.

HIS BENEVOLENCE.

> This only can the bliss bestow
> Immortal souls should prove;
> From one short word all pleasures flow,
> That blessed word is—Love.

If ever man rejoiced in the divine administration, and cordially endeavoured to imitate it by doing good, George Washington was that man. Taught by religion that " God is love," he wisely concluded those the most happy who love the most ; and, taught by experience that it is love alone that gives a participation and interest in others, capacitating us to rejoice with those who rejoice, and to weep with those who weep, he early studied that benevolence which rendered him so singularly the delight of mankind.

The marquis De Chastellux, who visited him in camp, tells us that " he was astonished and delighted to see the great American living among his officers and men as a father among his children, who at once revered and loved him with a filial tenderness."

. Brissot, another famous French traveller, assures us, that "throughout the continent every body spoke of Washington as of a father."

The dearest and best of all appellations, "The father of his country," was the neutral fruit of that benevolence which he so carefully cultivated through life. A singular instance of which we meet with in 1754, and the 22nd year of his age.

He was stationed at Alexandria with his regiment, the only one in the colony, and of which he was colonel. There happened at this time to be an election in Alexandria for members of the assembly : and the contest ran high between Colonel George Fairfax, and Mr. Elzey. Washington was the warm friend of Fairfax: and a Mr. Payne headed the friends of Elzey. A dispute happening to take place in the court-house yard, Washington, a thing very uncommon with him, became warm; and, which was still more uncommon, said something that offended Payne; whereupon the little gentleman, who, though but a cub in size, was the old lion in heart, raised his sturdy hickory, and, at a single blow, brought our hero to the ground. Several of Washington's officers being present, whipped out their cold irons in an instant: and it was believed that there would have been murder off-hand. To make bad worse, his regiment, hearing how he had been treated, bolted out from their barracks, with every man his weapon in his hand, threatening dreadful vengeance on those who had dared to knock down their beloved colonel. Happily for Mr. Paine and his party, Washington recovered, time enough to go out and meet his enraged soldiers : and, after thanking them for this expression of their love, and assuring them that he was not hurt in the least, he begged them, as they loved him or their duty, to return peaceably to their barracks. As for himself, he went to his room, generously chastising his imprudence, which had thus struck up a spark that had like to have thrown the

18

whole town into a flame. Finding on mature reflection, that he had been the aggressor, he resolved to make Mr. Payne honourable reparation, by asking his pardon on the morrow! No sooner had he made this noble resolution, than, recovering that delicious gaiety which accompanies good purposes in a virtuous mind, he went to a ball that night, and behaved as pleasantly as though nothing had happened! Glorious proof, that great souls, like great ships, are not affected by those little puffs which would overset feeble minds with passion, or sink them with spleen!

The next day he went to a tavern, and wrote a polite note to Mr. Payne, whom he requested to meet him. Mr. Payne took it for a challenge, and repaired to the tavern, not without expecting to see a pair of pistols produced. But what was his surprise on entering the chamber, to see a decanter of wine and glasses on the table! Washington arose, and in a very friendly manner met him; and gave him his hand. "Mr. Payne," said he, "to err is nature: to rectify error is glory. I find I was wrong yesterday: but I wish to be right to-day. You have had some satisfaction: and if you think that sufficient, here's my hand; let us be friends."

Admirable youth! Noble speech! No wonder, since it charms us so, that it had such an effect on Mr. Payne, who from that moment became the most ardent admirer and friend of Washington, and ready at any time, for his sake, to charge up to a battery of two and forty pounders.

What a lesson for our young countrymen! Had Washington been one of the race of little men, how sadly different would have been his conduct on this occasion! Instead of going that night to the ball, and acting the lively agreeable friend, he would, like an angry viper that had been trod on, have retired to his chamber. There he would have found no such entertainment as Washington had at this ball; no sprightly music, no delicious wines, no sweetly

smiling friends. On the contrary, all the tortures of
a soul brooding over its indignities, until reflection
had whipped it up into pangs of rage unutterable,
while all the demons of hell, with blood-stained
torches pointing at his bleeding honour, cried out
" revenge ! revenge !. revenge !" There in his chamber, he would have passed the gloomy night preparing his pistols, moulding his bullets, or with furious
looks driving them through the body of his enemy
chalked on the wall. The next morning would have
seen him on the field, and in language lately heard
in this state, calling out to his hated antagonist, You
have injured me, sir, beyond reconciliation : and by
—— I'll kill you if I can. While his antagonist, in a
style equally musical and christian, would have
rejoined, Kill, and be——! Pop go the pistols—
down tumbles one of the combatants; while the
murderer, with knocking knees and looks of Cain,
flies from the avenger of blood ! The murdered man
is carried to his house, a ghastly, bloody corpse.
Merciful God ! what a scene ensues ! some are stu-
pified with horror ! others sink lifeless to the floor !
His tender sisters, wild shrieking with despair, throw
themselves on their dead brother and kiss his ice-cold
lips ; while his aged parents, crushed under unutterable woe, go down in their snowy locks broken-
hearted to the grave.

Thus bloody and miserable might have been the
end of Washington or of Payne, had Washington
been one of those poor deluded young men, who are
determined to be great ; and so be brought forward
in newspapers, in spite of God or devil. But Washington was not born to exemplify those horrid tragedies, which cowards create in society by pusillani-
mously giving way to their bad passions. No—he
was born to teach his countrymen what sweet peace
and harmony might for ever smile in the habitations
of men, if all had but the courage, like himself, to
obey the sacred voice of justice and humanity. By

firmly obeying these, he preserved his hands unstained by the blood of a fellow man; and his soul unharrowed by the cruel tooth of never-dying remorse. By firmly obeying these, he preserved a life, which, crowned with deeds of justice and benevolence, has brought more glory to God, more good to man, and more honor to himself, than any life ever spent since the race of man began.

Sons of Columbia! would you know what is true courage? see it defined, see it exemplified in this act of your young but great countryman. Never man possessed a more undaunted courage, than Washington. But in him this noble quality was the lifeguard of his reason, not the assassin; a ready servant to obey her commands, not a bully to insult them; a champion to defend his neighbour's rights, not a tyrant to invade them. Transported by sudden passion, to which all are liable, he offended Mr. Payne, who resented it rather too roughly, by knocking him down on the spot. Washington had it in his power to have taken ample revenge: and cowards, who have no command over their passions, would have done it. But duty forbade him: and he had the courage to obey. Reason whispered the folly of harbouring black passions in his soul, poisoning his peace. He instantly banished them; and went to a ball, to drink sweet streams of friendship from the eyes of happy friends. Again reason whispered him, that having been the aggressor, he ought to ask Payne's pardon, and compromise the difference with him. In this also he had the courage to obey her sacred voice.

. In what history, ancient or modern, sacred or profane, can you find, in so young a man, only twenty-two, such an instance of that TRUE HEROIC VALOUR which combats malignant passions—conquers unreasonable self—rejects the hell of hatred, and invites the heaven of love into our own bosoms, and into those of our brethren with whom we may have

quarrelled? Joseph forgiving his brethren in the land
of Egypt; David sparing that inveterate seeker of
his life, Saul; Sir Walter Raleigh pardoning the
young man who spit in his face; afford, it is true,
charming specimens of the sublime and beautiful in
action: certainly, such men are worthies of the
world, and brightest ornaments of human nature.
But yet none of them have gone beyond Washington
in the affair of Payne.

A few years after this, Payne had a cause tried in
Fairfax court. Washington happened on that day
to be in the house. The lawyer on the other side,
finding he was going fast to leeward, thought he
would luff up with a whole broadside at Payne's
character: and, after raking him fore and aft with
abuse, he artfully bore away under the lee of the
jury's prejudices, which he endeavoured to inflame
against him. "Yes, please your worships," continued he, "as a proof that this Payne is a most
turbulent fellow, and capable of all I tell you, be
pleased to remember, gentlemen of the jury, that
this is the very man, who some time ago treated
our beloved colonel Washington so barbarously.
Yes, this is the wretch, who dared, in this very
court-house yard, to lift up his impious hand against
that greatest and best of men, and knocked him down
as though he had been a bullock of the stalls.

This, roared in a thundering tone, and with a tremendous stamp on the floor, made Payne look very
dejected; for he saw the countenance of the court
beginning to blacken on him. But Washington rose
immediately, and thus addressed the bench:

"As to Mr. Payne's character, may it please your
worships," said he, "we all have the satisfaction to
know that it is perfectly unexceptionable: and with
respect to the little difference which formerly happened between that gentleman and myself, it was
instantly made up: and we have lived on the best
terms ever since: moreover, I wish all my acquaint-
18*

ance to know, that I entirely acquit Mr. Payne of
blame in that affair, and take it all on myself as the
aggressor."

Payne used often to relate another anecdote of
Washington, which reflects equal honour on the
goodness of his heart.

Immediately after the war," said he, " when the
conquering hero was returning in peace to his home,
with the laurels of victory green and flourishing on
his head, I felt a great desire to see him, and so set
out for Mount Vernon. As I drew near the house,
I began to experience a rising fear, lest he should
call to mind the blow I had given him in former
days. However, animating myself, I pushed on.
Washington met me at the door with a smiling welcome, and presently led me into an adjoining room,
where Mrs. Washington sat. "Here, my dear,"
said he, prsenting me to his lady, "here is the little
man you have so often heard me talk of; and who,
on a difference between us one day, had the resolution, to knock me down, big as I am. I know you
will honour him as he deserves; for I assure you he
has the heart of a true Virginian." " He said this,"
continued Mr. Payne, " with an air which convinced
me that his long familiarity with war had not robbed
him of a single spark of the goodness and nobleness of
his heart. And Mrs. Washington looked at him, I
thought, with a something in her eyes, which showed
that he appeared to her greater and lovelier than
ever."

A good tree, saith the divine teacher, bringeth forth
good fruit. No wonder then that we meet with so
many and such delicious fruits of CHARITY in Washington, whose soul was so rich in benevolence.

In consequence of his wealth and large landed
possessions, he had visits innumerable from the poor.
Knowing the great value of time and of good tempers
to them, he could not bear that they should lose
either, by long waiting and shuffling, and blowing

their fingers at his door. He had a room set apart for the reception of such poor persons as had business with him: and the porter had orders to conduct them into it, and to inform him immediately. And so affectionately attentive was he to them, that if he was in company with the greatest characters on the continent, when his servant informed him that a poor man wished to speak to him, he would instantly beg them to excuse him for a moment, and go and wait on him.

Washington's conduct showed that he disliked another practice, too common among some great men, who, not having the power to say, yes, nor the heart to say no, to a poor man, are fain to put him off with a "come again; come again;" and thus trot him backwards and forwards, wasting his time, wearing out his patience and shoes, and after all give him the mortification of a disappointment.

Washington could not be guilty of such cruel kindness. If he could not oblige a poor applicant, he would candidly tell him so at once: but then the goodness of his heart painted his regret so sensibly on his countenance, that even his refusals made him friends.

A poor Irishman, wanting a small farm, and hearing that Washington had one to rent, waited on him. Washington told him that he was sincerely sorry that he could not assist him; for he had just disposed of it. The poor man took his leave, but not without returning him a thousand thanks! Ah, do you thank me so heartily for a refusal! "Yes, upon my shoul, now plase your excellency's honour, and I do thank you a thousand times. For many a great man would have kept me waiting like a black negro. But your excellency's honour has told me straight off hand that you are sorry and God bless you for it, that you can't help me—and so your honour has done my business for me, in no time, and less."

The Potomac abounds with the finest herrings in

the world, which, when salted, furnish not only to
the wealthy a charming relish for their tea and coffee,
but also to the poor a delicious substitute for bacon.
But, fond as they are of this small boned bacon, as
they call it, many of them have not the means to
procure it.   Washington's heart felt for these poor
people; and provided a remedy. He ordered a seine
and a batteau to be kept on one of the best fishing
shores, on purpose for the poor. If the batteau were
lost, or the seine spoilt, which was often the case, he
had them replaced with new ones immediately. And
if the poor who came for fish were too weak handed
to haul the seine themselves, they needed but to apply to the overseer, who had orders from Washington to send hands to help them.   Thus all the poor
had it in their power to come down in the season,
and catch the finest fish for themselves and their
families. In what silver floods were ever yet caught
the herrings, which could have given to Washington
what he tasted, on seeing the poor driving away
from his shores, with carts laden with delicious fish,
and carrying home, whooping and singing to their
smiling wives and children, the rich prize, a whole
year's plenty.

In all his charities, he discovered great judgment
and care in selecting proper objects.   Character was
the main chance. Mount Vernon had no charms for
lazy, drunken, worthless beggars.   Persons of that
description knew very well that they must take their
application elsewhere. He never failed to remind
them of the great crime of robbing the public of their
services, and also the exceeding cruelty and injustice
of snapping up from the really indigent, what little
charity bread was stirring. But if the character
were good—if the poor petitioner were a sober,
honest, and industrious person, whom Providence
had by sickness or losses reduced to want—he found
a brother in Washington. It is incredible what
quantities of wool, corn, bacon, flour, clothes, &c.

were annually distributed to the poor, from the almost exhaustless heap, which the blessings of Heaven bestowed on this, its industrious and faithful steward.

"I had orders," said Mr. Peake, a sensible, honest manager of one of Washington's plantations, to fill a corn-house every year, for the sole use of the poor in my neighbourhood! to whom it was a most seasonable and precious relief; saving numbers of poor women and children from miserable famine, and blessing them with a cheerful plenteousness of bread." Mr. Lund Washington, long a manager of his Mount Vernon estate, had similar orders. One year when corn was so dear (a dollar per bushel) that numbers of the poor were on the point of starving, Mr. L. Washington, by order of the general, not only gave away all that could be spared from the granaries, but bought at that dear rate, several hundred bushels for them!

Anecdote of Washington.—The town of Alexandria, which now flourishes like a green bay tree, on the waters of the Potomac, was, 50 years ago, but a small village. But though small, it was lovely. Situated on the fine plain which banks the western margin of the river, and with snow white domes glistening through the trees that shook their green heads over the silver flood, it formed a view highly romantic and beautiful. Hence the name of the place at first was Bellhaven. But, with all the beauties to the eye, Bellhaven had no charms for the palate. Not that the neighbourhood of Bellhaven was a desert; on the contrary, it was, in many places, a garden spot abounding with luxuries. But its inhabitants, though wealthy, were not wise. By the successful culture of tobacco they had made money. And having filled their coach-houses with gilt carriages, and their dining rooms with gilt glasses, they began to look down on the poorer sort, and to talk about families. Of course it would never do for such

great people to run market carts!! Hence the poor
Bellhavenites, though embosomed in plenty were
often in danger of gnawing their nails; and unless
they could cater a lamb from some goodnatured
peasant, or a leash of chickens from the Sunday
negroes, were obliged to sit down with long faces to
a half-graced dinner of salt meat and Johnny cake.
This was the order of the day, A. D. '59, when
Washington, just married to the wealthy young Mrs.
Custis, had settled at Mount Vernon, nine miles
below Bellhaven. The unpleasant situation of the
families at that place soon reached his ear. To a
man of his character, with too much spirit to follow
a bad example, when he had the power to set a good
one, and too much wit to look for happiness any
where but in his own bosom, it could not long be
questionable what part he had to act. A market
cart was instantly constructed; and regularly, three
times a week, sent off to Bellhaven, filled with nice
roasters, kidney covered lamb and veal, green geese,
fat ducks, chickens by the basket, fresh butter, new
laid eggs, vegetables, and fruit of all sorts. Country
gentlemen, dining with their friends in town, very
soon marked the welcome change of diet. "Bless
us all!" exclaimed they, "what's the meaning of
this? you invited us to family fare, and here you've
given us a lord mayor's feast." "Yes," replied the
others, "thank God for sending Colonel Washington
into our neighbourhood." Thus, it was discovered,
to the extreme mortification of some of the little great
ones, that Colonel Washington should ever have run
a market cart!! But the better sort, who generally,
thank God, have sense enough to be led right, provided they can get a leader, soon fell into the track:
and market carts were soon seen travelling in abundance to town with every delicacy of the animal and
vegetable republics.

Thus the hungry wall which pride had raised
against Bellhaven was happily demolished. A flood-

tide of blessings rolled in from the neighbouring
country. The hearts of the merchants felt a fresh
pulse of love for their brothers, the farmers: and
even the little children, with cheeks red as the apples
they seized, were taught to lisp the praises of God.
And all this, reader, through the active benevolence
of one man.

The following anecdote was related to me by his
excellency Governor Johnson (Maryland,) one of the
few surviving heroes of '76.

"You seem, sir," said he addressing himself to me,
"very fond of collecting anecdotes of Gen. Washington. Well, I'll tell you one, to which you may
attach the most entire faith; for I have heard it a
dozen times and oftener, from the lips of a very
valuable man and a magistrate, in Conostoga, a Mr.
Conrad Hogmyer." "Just before the revolutionary
war," said Mr. Hogmyer, "I took a trip for my
health's sake to the Sweet Springs of Virginia, where
I found a world of people collected; some, like me,
looking for health, others for pleasure. In consequence of the crowd, I was at first rather hard run
for lodgings; but at length was lucky enough to get
a mattrass in the hut of a very honest baker of my
acquaintance, who often visited the springs for the
benefit of his oven. Being the only man of the trade
on the turf, and well skilled in the science of dough,
he met with no small encouragement: and it was
really a subject of surprize to see the heaps of English
loaves. Indian pones, French bricks, cakes, and
crackers, which lay piled on his counter every
morning. I often amused myself in marking the
various airs and manners of the different waiters,
who, in gay liveries and shining faces, came every
morning, rattling down their silver, and tripping
away with their bread by the basket. Among those
gay looking sons and daughters of Africa, I saw
every now and then, a poor Lazarite, with sallow
cheek and hollow eye, slowly creeping to the door,
and at a nod from the baker, eagerly seize a fine loaf

and bear it off without depositing a cent. Surely, thought I to myself, this baker must be the best man, or the greatest fool in the world. But fearing that this latter cap best fitted his pericranium, I one morning could not help breaking my mind to him, for crediting his bread to such very unpromising dealers. "Stophel," for that was his name, "you seem," said I, "to sell a world of bread here every day; but, notwithstanding that, I fear you don't gain much by it."

"No! 'squire? What makes you think so?"

"You credit too much, Stophel."

"Not I indeed, sir, not I. I don't credit a penny."

"Ay! how do you make that out, Stophel, don't I see the poor people every day carrying away your bread, and yet paying you nothing?"

"Pshaw, no matter for that, 'squire. They'll pay me all in a lump at last."

"At last! At last! Oh ho, at the last day, I suppose you mean, Stophel; when you have the conscience to expect that God Almighty will stand paymaster, and wipe off all your old scores for you, at a dash."

"Oh no! 'squire, we poor bakers can't give such long credit! but I'll tell you how we work the matter. The good man Colonel George Washington is here. Every season as soon as he comes, he calls and says to me, 'Stophel, you seem to have a great deal of company; and some, I fear, who don't come here for pleasure, and yet, you know, they can't do without eating. Though pale and sickly, they must have bread. But it will never do to make them pay for it. Poor creatures! they seem already low spirited enough through sickness and poverty. Their spirits must not be sunk lower by taking from them every day what little money they have pinched from their poor families at home. I'll tell you what's to be done, Stophel. You must give each of them a good hot loaf every morning; and charge it to me. When I am going away, I'll pay you all.'

And believe me, 'squire, he has often, at the end of the season, paid me as much as 80 dollars, and that too for poor creatures who did not know the hand that fed them; for I had strict orders from him not to mention a syllable of it to any body."

But though so kind to the bodies, Washington was still more kind and costly in his charities to the minds of the poor. Sensible that a republican government, that is, a government of the people, can never long subsist where the minds of the people are not enlightened, he earnestly recommended it to the citizens of the United States, to promote, as an object of primary importance, institutions for the general diffusion of knowledge. In this, as indeed in all other cases where any thing great or good was to be done, Washington led the way.

He established a charity school in Alexandria, and endowed it with a donation of four thousand dollars. The interest was regularly paid and expended on the education of fifteen boys. My young friend, the reverend Mr. Wiley, who, for talents, taste, and classical erudition, has few superiors in America, was educated by Washington.

In 1785, the assembly of his native state, Virginia, "desirous to embrace," as they said, "every suitable occasion of testifying their sense of the unexampled merits of George Washington, Esq.," presented him with fifty shares in the Potomac, and one hundred shares in the James River Navigation Company; making, in the whole, the important sum of ten thousand pounds sterling!

Of this public act, they requested the governor to transmit Washington a copy. In answer he addressed a letter to the governor, in which, "I take the liberty," says he, "of returning to the general assembly, through your hands, the profound and grateful acknowledgments inspired by so signal a mark of their beneficent intentions towards me."

He goes on to beg that they would excuse his,

determined resolution not to accept a farthing of it for his own use—" But," continued he, " if it should please the general assembly to permit me to turn the destination of the fund vested in me, from my private emolument, to objects of a public nature, it shall be my study, in selecting, to prove the sincerity of my gratitude for the honour conferred on me, by preferring such as may appear most subservient to the enlightened and patriotic view of the legislature."

They were cheerfully submitted to his disposal; and, according to promise, he appropriated them to works of the greatest utility: viz: his shares in James River canal, to a college in Rockbridge county, near the waters of James River; and his Potomac shares to a national university, to be erected in the federal district, on the great Potomac.

How noble and disinterested were his wishes for the good of his country! As if incapable of being satisfied with all that he had done for her while living, he endeavoured, by founding those noble institutions for the diffusion of knowledge and virtue, to make himself her benefactor when he should cease to live in this sublunary world.

Since the idea is perfectly correct, that the great Governor of the world must look with peculiar benignity on those of his children who most nearly resemble him in benevolence, may we not indulge the pleasing hope, that these colleges, founded by such a hand, shall prove the nurseries of the brightest genius and virtue; and that from their sacred halls will proceed in endless succession, the mighty Washingtons, and Jeffersons, the Franklins and Madisons of future times! O that Columbia may live before God! and that the bright days of her prosperity may never have an end!

Washington's behaviour to the generous Fayette ought never to be forgotten.

When that glorious young nobleman heard that Lord North had passed against America the decree of slavery; and that the American farmers with their rusty firelocks and pitchforks, in front of their shrieking wives and children, were inch by inch disputing the soil against a hireling soldiery, the tears gushed from his eyes. He tore himself from the arms of the loveliest, fondest of wives; flew to his sovereign for permission to fight; turned into powder and arms every livre that he could raise; and, in a swift sailing frigate rushing through the waves to America, presented himself before Washington. Washington, received him as his son, and gave him command, Under the eye of that hero he fought and conquered. Having aided to fix the independence of strangers, he hastened back to France, to liberate his own countrymen from the curses of monarchy; and to give them, like America, the blessings of a republic. A pupil of the temperate and virtuous Washington, he soon offended the hot headed demagogues of France. Banished from his native country, he was presently thrown, by royal jealousy, into a foreign prison. Most of us here in America, on hearing of his misfortunes, felt the kindly touch of sympathy. But alas! like those good people in the parable, we were so taken up with "buying land, trying oxen, or marrying wives," that we forgot our noble friend. But Washington did not forget him. His thoughts were often with him in his gloomy cell. He sent him a present of a thousand guineas—and in a letter to the Emperor of Germany, with equal delicacy and feeling, solicited his discharge, and permission to come to America. The letter concluded with these remarkable words:—"As it is a maxim with me never to ask what, under similar circumstances, I would not grant, your majesty will do me the justice to believe, that this request appears to me to correspond, with those great principles of magnanimity and wisdom which form the basis of sound policy and durable glory."

This letter produced, in part, the desired effect

For immediately after the receipt of it, the marquis experienced a great increase of attention; and in a short time he was liberated. Such was the respect paid to our American farmer, by one of the greatest monarchs in Europe.

In 1795, the marquis's son made his escape from France, and arrived at Boston. Soon as Washington heard of it, he sent his parental respects to the youth, and informed him, that, though, from motives of tenderness to his mother, who was in the power of the directory, he could not be seen publicly to notice him, yet he begged to be considered by him as his father and protector—advised him to enter as a student in the university near Boston, and to draw on him for whatever moneys he should want.

Congress, on hearing that a son of the noble marquis was in America, felt a deep interest in the youth, and ordered an immediate inquiry into his situation, intending generous things for him out of the national treasury. But finding that on this, as on all other occasions, Washington had done honour to the American name, they rejoiced exceedingly, and let the matter drop.

CHAPTER XV.

WASHINGTON'S CHARACTER CONCLUDED.

HIS INDUSTRY.

> Awake, my boy! and let the rising sun
> Blush to see his vigilance outdone;
> In cheerful works consume the fleeting day,
> Toil thy pleasure, and business all thy play.

But of all the virtues that adorned the life of this great man, there is none more worthy of our imitation than his admirable industry. It is to this virtue in her Washington, that America stands indebted for services past calculation : and it is from this virtue, that Washington himself snatched a wreath of glory that will never fade away. O that the good genius of America may prevail ! that the example of this, her favourite son, may be but universally adopted! Soon shall our land be free from all those sloth-begotten demons which now haunt and torment us. For whence do all our miseries proceed, but from lack of industry ! In a land like this, which heaven has blessed above all lands—a land abounding with the fish and flesh pots of Egypt, and flowing with the choicest milk and honey of Canaan—a land where the poorest Lazarus may get his fifty cents a day for the commonest labour—and buy the daintiest bread of corn flour for a cent a pound ! why is any man hungry, or thirsty, or naked, or in prison ? why but through his unpardonable sloth ?

But alas ! what would it avail, though the blest shade of Washington were to descend from his native skies, and with an angel's voice, recommend industry as the handmaid of health, wealth, innocence, and happiness to man. A notion, from the land of lies, has taken too deep root among some, that " labour is a low-lived thing, fit for none but poor people and slaves ! and that dress and pleasure are the only accomplishments for a gentleman ! But does it become a gentleman to saunter about, living on the charity of his relations—to suffer himself to be dunned by creditors, and, like a hunted wolf, to fly from the face of sheriffs and constables? Is it like a gentleman to take a generous woman from her parents, and reduce her to beggary—to see even her bed sold from under her, and herself and weeping infants turned out of doors ? It is like a gentleman to reduce one's children to rags, and to drive them like birds of heaven, to hedges and highways, to pick berries, filling their pale bloated bodies with disease ? Or is it like a gentleman to bring up one's sons in sloth, pleasure, and

dress, as young noblemen, and then leave them without estates, profession, or trades, to turn gamblers,
sharpers, or horse thieves? "From such gentlemen,
oh save my country, Heaven!" was Washington's
perpetual prayer, the emphatical prayer of his life and
great example! In his ear, wisdom was heard inces-
santly calling aloud, "He is the real gentleman, who
cheerfully contributes his every exertion to accomplish
heaven's favourite designs, the beauty, order and happiness of human life; whose industry appears in a
plentiful house and smiling wife; in the decent ap-
parel of his children, and in their good education
and virtuous manners; who is not afraid to see any
man on earth; but meets his creditors with a smiling
countenance, and with the welcome music of gold
and silver in his hand; who exerts an honest industry for wealth, that he may become as a water-course
in a thirsty land, a source of refreshment to a thous-
and poor."

This was the life, this the example set by Washington. His whole inheritance was but a small tract
of poor land in Stafford county, and a few negroes.
This appearing utterly insufficient for those purposes
of usefulness, with the charms of which his mind
seems to have been early smitten, he resolved to make
up the deficiency by dint of industry and economy.—
For these virtues, how excellent! how rare in youth!
Washington was admirably distinguished when but
a boy. At a time when many young men have no
higher ambition than a fine coat and a frolic, "often
have I seen him (says the reverend Mr. Le Massey)
riding about the country with his surveying instruments at his saddle," enjoying the double satisfaction
of obliging his fellow citizens by surveying their
lands, and of making money, not meanly to hoard,
but generously to lend to any worthy object that
asked it. This early industry was one of the first
steps to Washington's preferment. It attracted on
him the notice and admiration of his numerous ac-

quaintance, and, which was still more in his favour, it gave such uncommon strength to his constitution, such vigour to his mind, such a spirit for adventure, that he was ready for any glorious enterprize, no matter how difficult or dangerous. Witness the expedition from Williamsburg through the Indian country to the Ohio, which at the green age of twenty-one, he undertook for Governor Dinwiddie. Indeed this uncommon attachment to industry and useful life, made such an impression on the public mind in his favour, that by the time he was one and twenty he was appointed major and adjutant-general of the Virginia forces in the Northern Neck!

. There was at this time a young fellow in Williamsburg by the name of Jack B———, who possessed considerable vivacity, great good-nature, and several accomplishments of the bon companion sort. He could tell a good story, sing agreeably, scrape a little on the fiddle, and cut as many capers to the tune of old Roger, as any buck a-going; and being, besides, a young fellow of fortune, and a son of an intimate acquaintance, Jack was a great favourite of the governor, and much at his house. But all this could not save poor Jack from the twinges of envy. For, on hearing every body talk in praise of Major Washington, he could not help saying one day at the governor's table, "I wonder what makes the people so wrapped up in major Washington: I think, begging your excellency's pardon, I had as good a right to a major's commission." "Ah, Jack," replied the governor, "when we want diversion, we send for you. But when we want a man of business, we send for Major Washington."

Never was the great Alfred more anxious to improve his time than our Washington: and it appears that, like Alfred, he divided his time into four grand departments, sleep, devotion, recreation, and business. On the hours of buisness, whether in his own or his country's service, he would allow nothing to infringe.

While in camp, no company, however illustrious—
no pleasures, however elegant—no conversation, however agreeable—could prevail on him to neglect his
business. The moment that his hour of duty was
come, he would fill his glass, and with a smile, call
out his friends around the social board, "well, gentlemen, here is bon repos," and immediately with-
draw to business. Bon repos is a French cant for
good night. Washington drank it as a signal to break
up ; for the moment the company had swallowed the
general's bon repos, it was hats and off. General
Wayne, who, happily for America, understood fighting better than French, had some how or other taken
up a notion, than this same bon repos, to whom
Washington made such conscience of giving his last
bumper, must have been some great warrior of the
times of old. Having, by some extraordinary luck,
gotten hold of two or three dozen of good old wine,
he invited a parcel of hearty fellow-officers to dine
with him, and help him to break them to the health
of America. Soon as the cloth was removed, and
the bottles on the table, the hero of Stony Point cried
out, "come my brave fellows, fill your glass; here's
old bon repos for ever." The officers were thunderstruck : but having tured off their wine, rose up, one
and all to go. "Hey day! what'sall this, gentlemen?
what's all this?" "Why," replied they, did not you
drink bon repos, or good night?"

"What! is that the meaning of it?" "Yes," "Oh!
then, damn old bon repos, and take your seats again :
'or, by the life of Washington, you shan't stir a peg
till we have started every drop of our wine."

While he was employed in choosing a place on
the Potomac, for the federal city, his industry was
no less remarkable. Knowing how little is generally
done before breakfast, he made it a rule to rise so
early as to have breakfast over, and be on horseback
by the time the sun was up. Let the rising genera-
tion remember that he was then sixty years of age!

On his farm, his husbandry of time was equally exemplary. He contemplated a great object: an object worthy of Washington. He aimed at teaching his countrymen the art of enriching their lands, and consequently of rendering the condition of man and beast more plentiful and happy. He had seen thousands of acres, which, by constant cultivation, had lost the power of covering their nakedness even with a suit of humble sedge. He had seen thousands of wretched cattle, which, driven out houseless and hayless into the cold wintry rains, presented such trembling spectacles of starvation and misery, as were enough to start the tear into Pity's eye. To remedy these cruel evils (which certainly they are, for He who lent us these animals never meant that we should make their lives a curse to them, much less to our children, hardened by such daily sights of misery,) Washington generously set himself to make artificial meadows; to cultivate fields of clover; and to raise the most nutricious vegetables, such as cabbage, turnips, scarcity and potatoes; of which last article he planted in one year 700 bushels! To render these vast supplies of food the more beneficial to his cattle, he built houses of shelter for them all. "He showed me a barn," says Brissot, "upwards of 100 feet square, and of brick, designed as a store-house for his corn, potatoes, turnips, &c. around which he had constructed stables of an amazing length, for his cattle." Every one of them had a stall well littered with leaves or straw; and a rack and manger well furnished with hay and provender.

The pleasure and profits arising from such an arrangement are incalculable. How delicious must it have been to a man of Washington's feelings, to reflect that, even in the very worst weather, every creature, on his extensive farms, was warmly and comfortably provided; to have seen his numerous flocks and herds, gamboling around him through excess of joy, and fullness of fat; to have beheld his

steps washed with butter, and his dairies floated with
rivers of milk; to have seen his once naked fields and
frog-croaking swamps, now, by clearance or manure,
converted into meadows, standing thick with heavy
crops of timothy and sweet scented clover; while his
farm-yards were piled with such quantities of litter
and manure as afforded a constantly increasing fertility to his lands.

Here was an employment worthy of Washington;
an employment, which we might indeed have expected from him, who, through life, had studied the
best interests of his countrymen; who, first as a soldier, had defended them from slavery, and crowned
them with liberty; then, as a statesman, had preserved them from war, and secured to them the blessings of peace; and now as the last, but not the least
services of his life, was teaching them the great arts
of improving their farms, multiplying their cattle,
enriching their lands, and thus pouring a flood of
plenty and of comfort through the joyful habitations
of man and beast.

Full of the greatly benevolent idea, no wonder that
he was so frugal of his time. Though the most hospitable of all the hospitable Virginians, he would not
suffer the society of his dearest friends to take him
from his business. Long accustomed to find his
happiness in doing his duty, he had attained to such
a royal arch degree of virtue, as to be restless and
uneasy while his duty was neglected. Hence, of all
that ever lived, Washington was the most rigidly
observant of those hours of business which were
necessary to the successful management of his vast
concerns. "Gentlemen, (he would often say to his
friends who visited him) I must beg leave of absence
a few hours in the forenoon: here is plenty of amuse-
ments, books, music, &c. Consider yourselves at
home, and be happy." He came in about twelve
o'clock; and then, as if animated by the conscious-
ness of having done his duty, and that all was going

right, would give himself up to his friends and to
decent mirth the rest of the day.

But his mornings were always his own.   Long
before the sun peeped into the chambers of the slug-
gard, Washington was on horseback, and out among
his overseers and servants : and neither himself nor
any about him were allowed to eat the bread of idleness.   The happy effects of such industry were obvious.   Well manured and tilled, his lands yielded a
grateful return : and it was at once pleasing and astonishing to behold the immense quantities of fine hay,
of fat cattle, and choice grain, that were raised on his
farms ; of wheat 7000 bushels in one year, and 5000
bushels of Indian corn ! His servants fared plentiful-
ly.   His cattle never had the hollow horn.   And the
surplus of his prudence, sold to the merchants, furnished bread to the needy, and a revenue to himself more
than sufficient to defray his vast expenditures, and to
spread a table of true Virginian hospitality for those
crowds of friends and foreigners whom affection or
curiosity led to visit him.

Oh ! divine Industry ! queen mother of all our
virtues and of all our blessings ! what is there of
great or of good in this wide world that springs not
from thy royal bounty ? And thou, O ! infernal Sloth !
fruitful fountain of all our crimes and and curses !
what is there of mean or of miserable in the lot of
man that flows not from thy hellish malice ?

What was it that betrayed David, otherwise the
best of kings, into the worst of crimes ? Idleness.
Sauntering about idly on the terrace of his palace, he
beheld the naked beauties of the distant Bathsheba.
Lust, adultery, and murder were the consequences.

What was it that brought on a ten year's war between the Greeks and Trojans ? Idleness.   Young
Paris, the coxcomb of Troy, having nothing to do,
strolls over to the court of Menelaus (a Greek prince)
whose beauteous wife, Helen, the black-eyed queen
of love, he corrupts and carries off to Troy.   A

bloody war ensues.   Paris is slain.   His father, brothers, and myriads of wretched subjects are slaugh-
tered: and Troy, the finest city of Asia, is reduced
to ashes!

What was it that hurried poor Mr. A——d to that
horrid act of suicide, which froze the blood of all who
heard it? Idleness.   His young wife, with all that
we could conceive of sweetness, tenderness, and truth
in an angel's form; and his three beauteous babes
were the three graces in smiling infancy.   But oh,
wretched man! having nothing to do! he strolled to
a tavern, and to a card table, where he lost his all!
five thousand pounds, lately settled on him by a fond
father! He awakes to horrors unutterable!   What
will become of his ruined wife! his beggared babes?
Believing his torments little inferior to those of the
damned, he seizes the fatal pistol; drives the scorching bullet through his brains; and flies a shrieking
ghost to join the mournful throng!

O sad sight! see yon tall young man, in powder
and ruffles, standing before his judges, trembling like
an aspen, and pale and blank as the picture of guilt;
while the crowded court house, every countenance
filled with pity or contempt, is fixed upon him. Alas!
what could have brought him to this? Idleness. His
father happening to possess 500 acres of poor land,
and a few negroes, thought it would be an eternal
disgrace to his family to bring up his son, (though he
had many,) to be a mechanic.   No: he must be a
gentleman!!   Grown to man's estate, and having no
profession, trade, or habit of industry to support this
pleasant life, he took to horse-stealing.   If we had
leisure to wait, we should presently see this unhappy
youth, on receiving sentence of death, bursting into
sobs and cries sufficient to make us wish he had
never been born.   But let us leave these horrible
scenes of shame, misery, and death, into which idleness never fails to bring poor deluded youth, and
joyfully return to our beloved Washington, and

to his health, wealth, and glory-giving goddess, Industry.

What is it that braces the nerves, purifies the blood, and hands down the flame of life, bright and sparkling, to old age? What, but rosy checked Industry. See Washington so invigorated by constant exercise, that, though hereditarily subject to the gout, of which all his family died, he entirely escaped it; and, even at the age of 66, continued straight and active as a young grenadier, and ready once more at his country's call, to lead her eager warriors to the field.

What is it that preserves the morals of young men unsoiled, and secures the blessings of unblemished character and unbroken health? What, but snow-robed industry? See Washington under the guardianship of industry, walking the slippery paths of youth, safe and uncorrupted, though born in a country whose fertility and climate furnished both the means and invitation to vice. Early smitten with the love of glory; early engaged in the noble pursuit of knowledge, of independence, and of usefulness; he had no eyes to see bad examples, nor ensnaring objects; no ears to hear horrid oaths, nor obscene language; no leisure for impure passions nor criminal amours. Hence he enjoyed that purity of soul, which is rightly called its sunshine; and which impressed a dignity on his character, and gave him a beauty and loveliness in the eyes of men, that contributed more to his rise in the world, than young people can readily conceive.

And what is it that raises a young man from poverty to wealth, from obscurity to never-dying fame? What, but industry? See Washington, born of humble parents, and in humble circumstances—born in a narrow nook and obscure corner of the British plantations! yet lo! What great things wonder-working industry can bring out of this unpromising Nazareth. While but a youth, he mani-

fested such a noble contempt of sloth, such a manly
spirit to be always learning or doing something useful or clever, that he was the praise of all who knew
him. And, though but 15, so high were the hopes
entertained of him, he was appointed a surveyor!
arduous task! But his industry was a full match
for it. Such was the alertness with which he carried
on his survey; such the neatness and accuracy of his
plats and drafts, that he met with universal applause.
Full-fed and flushed with so much fare of praise, a
fare of all others the most toothsome and wholesome
to generous minds, our young eagle began to flap his
wings of honest ambition, and to pant for nobler
darings. A fair occasion was soon offered—a dangerous expedition through the Indian wilds, as
already mentioned, to the French Mamelukes on the
Ohio. Nobody else having ambition for such an
adventure, Washington's offer was gladly accepted.
And he executed that hazardous and important trust
with such diligence and propriety, that he received
the thanks of the governor and council. Honours
came down on him now in showers. He was appointed major and adjutant-general of the Virginia
forces; then a colonel; afterwards a member of the
house of burgesses; next, generalissimo of the armies
of the United States; and, finally, chief magistrate
of the Union. All these floods of prosperity and
honour, which in thousands would have but served
to bloat with lust or pride, with him served but the
more to rouse his industry, and to enlarge his usefulness; for such was his economy of time, and so
admirable his method and regularity of business, that
he always kept a-head of it.* No letters of conse-

---

* He was taken ill on Friday. An intimate friend asked him if he
wished to have any thing done on the arrangement of his temporal
affairs. He shook his head, and replied, "No, I thank you; for my
books are all posted to Tuesday!" That industry and method must
be truly astonishing, which in the management of possessions so vast
and complicated as his, kept every thing so harmoniously adjusted, as
to be ready, at a moment's warning, to leave the world for ever without a wish to alter a tittle.

quence were unanswered. No reasonable expectations were disappointed. No necessary information was ever neglected. Neither the congress, nor the governors of the several states, nor the officers of his army, nor the British generals, nor even the overseers and stewards on his farms, were uninformed what he expected from them. Nobody concerned with him was idle or fretted for want of knowing what to do.

O admirable man! O great preceptor to his country! no wonder every body honoured him who honoured every body; for the poorest beggar that wrote to him on business, was sure to receive a speedy and decisive answer. No wonder every body loved him, who, by his unwearied attention to the public good, manifested the tenderest love for every body. No wonder that his country delighted to honour him, who shewed such a sense of her honours that he would not allow even a leaf of them to wither; but so watered them all with the refreshing streams of industry, that they continued to bloom with ever-increasing glory on his head.

Since the day that God created man on the earth, none ever displayed the power of industry more signally than did George Washington. Had he, as prince of Wales, or as dauphin of France rendered such great services, or attained such immortal honours, it would not have seemed so marvellous in our eyes. But that a poor young man, with neither king, lords, nor commons to back him—with no princes, nor strumpets of princes, to curry favour for him—with no gold but his virtue, no silver but his industry, should, with this old-fashioned coin, have stolen away the hearts of all the American Israel, and from a sheep-cot have ascended the throne of his country's affections, and acquired a name above the mighty ones of the earth! this is marvellous indeed! It is surely the noblest panegyric ever yet paid to that great virtue, industry, which has "length of days in her right hand; and in her left hand riches and honours."

Young reader! go thy way; think of Washington; and HOPE. Though humble thy birth, low thy fortune, and few thy friends, still think of Washington; and HOPE. Like him, honour thy God; and delight in glorious toil. Then, like him, "thou shalt stand before kings. Thou shalt not stand before common men."

CHAPTER XVI.

WASHINGTON'S CHARACTER CONTINUED.

HIS PATRIOTISM.

" O eternal King of men and angels, elevate our minds! each low and partial passion thence dispel! till this great truth in every heart be known, that none but those who aid the public cause, can shield their country or themselves from chains."

LEONIDAS.

IN this grand republican virtue, we can with pleasure compare our Washington with the greatest worthies of ancient or modern times.

The patriotism of the Roman emperor, Alexander, has been celebrated through all ages, because he was never known to give any place through favour or friendship; but employed those only whom he believed to be the best qualified to serve his country. In our Washington we meet this great and honest emperor again. For in choosing men to serve his country, Washington knew no recommendation but merit—had no favourite but worth. No relations, however near—no friends, however dear—stood any chance for places under him, provided he knew men better qualified. Respecting such men, he never troubled himself to inquire, whether they were foreigners or natives, federalists or democrats. Some of the young officers of his native state, on hearing that colonel Washington was made COMMANDER IN CHIEF, were prodigiously pleased, expecting to be made field officers immediately. But in this they were so utterly mistaken, that some of them have foolishly said, "it was a misfortune to be a Virginian." Indeed, his great soul was so truly republican, that, during the whole of his administration, he was never known to advance an individual of his. own name and family.

The British, with good reason, admire and extol admiral Blake as one of the bravest and best of patriots; because, though he disliked Oliver Cromwell, yet he fought gallantly under him; and, with his dying breath, exhorted his men, "to love their country as a common mother; and, no matter what hands the government might fall into, to fight for her like good children."

Of the same noble spirit was Washington. Often was he called to obey men greatly his inferiors, and to execute orders which he entirely disapproved. But he was never known to falter. Sensible of the infinite importance of union and order to the good of his country, he ever yielded a prompt obedience to her delegated will. And, not content with setting us, through life, so fair an example, he leaves us at his death, this blessed advice: "Your government claims your utmost confidence and support. RESPECT for its AUTHORITY, compliance with its laws, acquiescence in its measures, are duties enjoined by the fundamental maxims of TRUE LIBERTY. The basis of our political system is the right of the people to make and alter their constitutions of government. But the constitution, which at any time exists, until changed by an explicit and authentic act of the whole people, is SACREDLY OBLIGATORY UPON ALL."

History has lavished its choicest praises on those magnanimous patriots, who, in their wars for liberty and their country, have cheerfully sacrificed their own wealth to defeat the common enemy.

Equal to this was the spirit of Washington. **For,** during the war, while he was with the army to the north, a British frigate came up the Potomac, to Mount Vernon ; and threatened to lay the place in ashes, if provisions were not instantly sent on board. To save that venerable mansion, the manager sent aboard the requisite supplies. On hearing the matter, Washington wrote his manager the following letter :

" Sir—It gives me extreme concern to hear that you furnished the enemy with refreshments. It would have been a less painful circumstance to me, to have heard, that in consequence of your non-compliance with their request, they had laid my plantation in ruins.

GEORGE WASHINGTON."

But, among all his splendid acts of patriotism, there is none which, with so little noise, may do us more good, than his " Legacy, or Farewell to the People of the United States." In this admirable bequest, like a true teacher sent from God, he dwells chiefly on our union and brotherly love. This, the first birth of true religion, appears to him as the one thing needful, the spring of political life, and bond of perfection.

On this topic he employs all the energies of his mind : and, in words worthy to be written in gold, emphatically beseeches his countrymen to guard with holiest care " the unity of the government," as the " main pillar and palladium of their liberty, their independence, and every thing most dear to them on earth."

Little did that illustrious patriot suspect, that, in so short a time after his death, the awful idea of disunion should have become familiar to the public eye !

—so familiar as to have worn off half its horrors from the minds of many of our deluded citizens ! Disunion! Merciful God ! what good man can think of it but as of treason, and as a very Pandora's box, replete with every curse that can give up our dear country to desolation and havoc !

This disorganizing scheme has been three times brought forward, by what Washington terms "cunning, ambitious, and unprincipled men," making use of a thousand arts to shut the eyes of the citizens on that yawning gulph to which they were so wickedly misleading them. And each time, Lucifer-like, these ministers of darkness have clothed themselves over as "angels of light" with the captivating plea of public good.—"The disadvantages of the union ! the disadvantages of the union ?" is their constant cry. Now admitting it to be true, that this so much hated union has its disadvantages, (and where is there any human institution, even the noblest, that is free from them ?) yet is it not the parent of blessings so many and great, that no good man, as Washington says, "can think of them without gratitude and rejoicing?" and is it not equally true, that these disadvantages of the union would not, in fifty years, equal the ruinous consequence of a disunion, in probably half a year.

At present,* the plea for this most horrible measure, is the mischievous effects of the embargo.— Well, grant that it is mischievous, highly mischievous and painful, for such we all feel it, yet how inexpressibly absurd it must be, to put the loss of trade, for a year or two, in competition with the peace and happiness, the independence and sovereignty of our country? Would not this be an act a thousand times more mad and wicked than that of the wretched Esau, who, to remove the cravings of a momentary appetite, sold his birth-right for a mess of pottage !

At this day, through the great mercies of God, we

* This was written Anno Domini, 1809.

have cause to consider ourselves the happiest nation
on earth.—List! oh list!

For many years past the greater part of Christendom has been involved in all the horrors of the most
bloody and destructive wars. Their kings and queens
have been rudely hurled from their thrones: and the
"honourable men and the princes," verifying the
mournful language of ancient prophecy, have been
seen embracing the dung-hill, or flying from their
distracted countries: while the mass of the people,
unable to fly, have been crushed to the earth with
tythes and taxes—with impressments and conscriptions—with forced loans and arbitrary requisitions—
with martial law, administered by military judges,
with the bayonet at the breast of the citizens! On
the other hand, during all these horrid convulsions
and miseries of other nations, we, thoughtless, thank-
less we, have enjoyed all the blessings of peace,
plenty, and security. Our persons have been free
from the violence of impressments and conscriptions;
and our lives and property perfectly safe under the
nightly staves of a few old watchmen! while other
nations have been over-run with devouring armies,
and doomed to see their houses in flames, and the
garments of their children rolled in blood, we, like
favoured Israel, have been sitting under our vine and
fig-tree, none daring to make us afraid. We have
been advancing in riches and strength, with a rapidity
unequalled in the history of man. We have been
progressing in arts, manufactures, and commerce, to
an extent and success that has astonished the most
enlightened Europeans: and even at this moment,
while suffering under the privations of the embargo,
we are feasted with every necessary, and enjoying
many of the elegancies of life.

And yet, with so many substantial blessings in our
hands, with so much heaven-sent manna in our mouths,
like ungrateful Israel, we are mourning for lack of
European luxuries (as they did for the Egyptian

flesh-pots,) luxuries which we once enjoyed, but are now most unjustly deprived of by our brethren, the nations of Europe, who are stronger than we. And as if that were not a sufficient evil—as if it were not grievous enough to suffer such a hindrance in trade, agriculture, and business of all kinds—we are now threatened with one, in comparison of which our present privations are insignificant—one which of all others, Washington most dreaded, and was most startled at, I mean a separation of the states, and consequently, civil war.

This dreadful consequence is as obvious as it is dreadful. Yes, it is most obvious, that the separation of the states can never take place without civil war. For if the states, disposed to separate, were unanimous in the attempt, the general government could not look idly on their apostacy, but must resist it! and to that end must call out the force of the rest of the union to crush it. And ,here, merciful God! what scenes are rising before the eyes of horror-struck imagination? A whole nation suddenly filled with terror; "men's hearts failing them for fear, and for looking to those things that are coming on the land" —the drums and instruments of war beginning to sound—the warriors' guns and swords preparing; not for cheerful defence of liberty and country, which would make war glorious; but for the gloomy and infernal work of civil discord. Sisters, mute with grief, and looking through swelling tears, on their brothers, as they gird on the hated swords—wives, shaking with strong fits, and, with their little children, filling their houses with lamentations for husbands and fathers tearing themselves away for the dismal war, whence they are to return no more! while aged parents, at parting with their sons, express the deep grief only in groans! or, wringing their withered hands, with tearful eyes to heaven, implore a speedy grave to put their griefs to rest.

But all this is but the beginning of sorrows. For

who can paint the scenes which ensue when the two armies meet? when they meet, not in the liberal spirit of stranger troops, who, fighting merely for honour and pay, are ready, in the first moment of victory, to sheath their swords, and to treat the vanquished with humanity and politeness; but in all the bitterness and exterminating spirit of a family quarrel, where men, after numberless acts of the blackest slander and of rancorous hate, having done every thing to destroy each other's souls, are now come together to destroy each other's bodies. Hence, the moment the ill-fated parties meet, their fierce revengeful passions take fire: scarce can they wait the trumpet's dreadful signal. Then, rushing on each other, more like demons than men, they thrust and stab, and shout and yell, in the horrid work of mutual slaughter.

And when one of the wretched parties, nearly consumed by the sword, and unable to resist any longer, cry for quarters, they cry in vain.

The furious conquerors feel not the touch of pity; but, regardless of uplifted hands and prayers, continue their cruel blows till all is hushed in death.

This is the horrid fate of all civil wars. The streets of ancient Rome; the fields of Culloden; the plains of modern France; and even the piney woods of Georgia and South Carolina, strewed with mangled carcases, all give awful proof, that when brethren turn their swords into each other's bowels, war degenerates into murder, and battles into butcheries.

Nor can even the grave set limits to their rage; but, like lions, turning from the mangled dead, they fly for new game to the living. All those, who by their wealth had most injured, or by their writings had most inflamed them, are sure to be the victims of their vengeance. Such persons—as was the case in the last war, between the whigs and tories in the southern states—have been dragged out of their houses, and, amidst the screams of their wives and children, have been hung up on the trees, or cut to pieces with swords with the most savage joy; while their furniture has been plundered, their houses burnt, their cattle and slaves carried off, and their widows and children driven out, crying, and without bread, into the barren woods.

Nor does this tragedy (of a free government madly divided and destroying itself) terminate here. Even this, as Solomon says, is but their "way to hell and their going down by the chambers of death," (political slavery.) For when nations thus wickedly abuse their liberty, God will take it away. When they will not live in peace, out of virtuous choice, they shall be compelled by brutal force.

And since they would not let God reign over them with a golden sceptre of reason and equal laws, he will set a master over them with a scourge of scorpions and an iron rod: some proud tyrant, who, looking on our country but as his estate, and ourselves as his cattle, shall waste our wealth on the pomps of his court, or the salaries of his officers; destroy our sons in his ambitious wars; and beggar us with exactions, as long as his ministers can invent taxes, or we, by hard labour, can raise money to pay them.

"Then," in the words of Washington, "what a triumph for the advocates of despotism, to find that we are incapable of governing ourselves; and that systems founded on equal liberty are ideal and fallacious!" Then, how will the proud sons of despotism shake themselves with laughter on their thrones; and hell itself, responsive to their joy, clank her congratulating chains, that heaven is defeated, and the misery of man is sealed.

But, O ye favoured countrymen of Washington! your republic is not yet lost; there is still hope. The arm that wrought your political salvation, is still stretched out to save; then hear his voice and live! Hear the voice of the Divine Founder of your republic: "Little children, love one another." Hear his

voice from the lips of his servant Washington:
"Above all things hold dear your national union.
Accustom yourselves to estimate its immense, its infinite value to your individual and national happiness.
Look on it as the palladium of your tranquillity at
home; of your peace abroad; of your safety; of
your prosperity; and even of that very liberty which
you so highly prize!" To this you are bound by
every tie of gratitude and love to God or man.   1st.
As to God, no people more than you can be bound
to adore that invisible hand which rules the affairs
of men. 'Twas he who fought your battles, and
against such fearful odds established your independence; and afterwards disposed your hearts for the
reception of a general and equal government. And
for what did God perform all these miracles for you,
but that he might glorify himself in your protection
and happiness? And will you now rise up with joy
to co-operate with God in the glorious work of beau-
tifying, with the fruits of righteousness, this goodly
land, which he has so honoured, that he may place
his own great name therein?

And remember, moreover, my countrymen, that
you are now the favoured actors on a most conspicuous theatre; a theatre which seems peculiarly
designated of Heaven for the display of human greatness and felicity. Far from the furious passions and
politics of Europe, you are placed here by yourselves,
the sole proprietors of a vast region, embracing all
the soils and climates of the earth, and abounding
with all the conveniences of life. And Heaven has
crowned all its blessings by giving you a freer
government and a fairer opportunity for political
happiness than any other nation was ever favoured
with. In this view, citizens of the United States, you
are certainly responsible for the highest trust ever
confided to any people. The eyes of long oppressed
humanity are now looking up to you as to her last
hope; the whole world are anxious spectators of

your trial; and with your behaviour at this crisis, not only your own, but the destiny of unborn millions is involved. If, now, you make a wise use of the all important opportunity—if your free constitution should be sacredly maintained—if honour, if patriotism, if union, and brotherly love should prevail, with all the good qualities which ennoble the character of nations—then the victory will be sure: your triumph will be complete: and the pressure of the present difficulties, instead of weakening will give a firmer tone to the federal government, that shall probably immortalize the blessings of LIBERTY to our children and children's children.

Then rouse! my generous countrymen, rouse! and, filled with the awfulness of our situation, with the glorious spirit of '76, rally around the sacred standard of your country. As good children give her all your support. Respect her authority!—comply with her laws! acquiesce in her measures! Thus cemented by love, she shall become like the precious wedge of Ophir that defies the furnace; and coming forth from the fiery trial brighter than ever, she shall shed on the cause of freedom, a dignity and lustre which it never enjoyed before; a lustre which cannot fail to have a favourable influence on the rights of man. Other nations, finding from your example, that men are capable of governing themselves, will aspire to the same honour and felicity. Great and successful struggles will be made for liberty. Free governments (the pure mothers of nations,) will at length be established. Honouring all their virtuous children alike, jealousies and hatreds will cease, and cordial love prevail, inviting the industry of all, the blessing of plenty will be spread abroad, and shameless thefts be done away. And wisdom and worth (as in the choice of a free people) being called to high places, errors will be rare. Vices, ashamed, shall hide their odious heads; cruelties seem abhorrent, and wars unknown. Thus, step by step progressing in virtue, the world will ripen for glory, till the great hour of her dissolution being come, the ready archangel shall lift his trumpet, and sound her knell. The last refining flames shall then kindle on this tear-bathed, blood-stained globe, while from its ashes a new earth shall spring, far happier than the first. There, freed from all their imperfections, the spirits of good men, (the only true patriots,) shall dwell together, and spend their ever brightening days in loves and joys eternal.

May the Great Founder of your holy republic keep you all under his divine protection; incline your hearts to cultivate a spirit of cheerful subordination to government; to entertain a brotherly affection and love for one another; and finally dispose you all to do justice; to love mercy; and to demean yourselves with that charity, humility, and pacific temper of mind, which were the characteristics of the Divine Author of our blessed religion; without an humble imitation of whose example, in these things, we can never hope to be a great and happy nation."

CONCLUSION.

WASHINGTON'S WILL.

Few great men are great in every thing. But in the last testament of this extraordinary American, we see some things altogether characteristic.

When Benedict Arnold came to die, he said—"I bequeath my soul to God."

When Henry Laurens, president of the first congress, came to die, he said, "My flesh is too good for worms: I give it to the flames;" which was done.

But Washington makes no preamble about his soul or body. As to his soul, having made it his great business to re-instamp on it the image of God, he doubted not but it would be remembered, when Christ should come "to make up his jewels."

And as to his body, that admirable piece of divine mechanism, so long the honoured servant of duty to his God and his country, he trusted, that, though "sown in dishonour, it would one day be raised in glory;" so leaving it to rest in hope, he proceeds to the following distribution of his worldly goods:

1st. Though an old husband of 68, yet, with the gallantry and warm affection of a young groom, he gives the whole of his estate (530,000 dollars) to his beloved wife Martha.

2d. Like a pure republican, he orders all his slaves to be liberated, at certain ages, on his wife's death—lamenting, that from obstacles insurmountable, he could not have done it earlier.

3d. He confirms his former donations, viz. 4000 dollars to a charity school in the town of Alexandria; 10,000 dollars to Liberty Hall Academy, Rockbridge county, Virginia; and 20,000 dollars to a national university, to be founded in Washington; with this remark: "It has always been a source of serious regret with me, to see the youth of these United States sent to foreign countries for education, often before their minds were formed, or they had imbibed just ideas of the happiness of their own; contracting too frequently, not only habits of dissipation and extravagance, but principles unfriendly to republican government, and to the true and genuine liberties of mankind.

"For these reasons, it has been my ardent wish to see a university in a central part of the union, to which the youth of fortune and talents, from all parts thereof, may be sent for the completion of their education in all the branches of polite and useful learning, and especially of politics and good government; and also that, by associating with each other, and forming friendships in early life, they may be

enabled to free themselves from those local prejudices and state jealousies, which are never-failing
sources of disquietude to the public mind, and pregnant with mischievous consequences to this country."

4th. Having no children, he bequeaths the whole
of his estate, a few legacies excepted, to the children,
23 in number, of his brothers and sister; and, like a
generous and affectionate relative, he gave to the
children of his half brother, Augustin, equally as to
those of his own brothers. And, 'tis a most pleasing
fact, he gave to his wife's grand-children in like
liberal measure with his own nieces and nephews!
the part given to each has been computed at 20,000
dollars.

FINIS.

CPSIA information can be obtained
at www.ICGtesting.com
Printed in the USA
LVHW080029270123
738009LV00004B/120

9 781375 684514